I0120179

Delivering Quality Services to All in Alentejo

PREPARING REGIONS FOR DEMOGRAPHIC CHANGE

OECD

BETTER POLICIES FOR BETTER LIVES

This document, as well as any data and map included herein, are without prejudice to the status of or sovereignty over any territory, to the delimitation of international frontiers and boundaries and to the name of any territory, city or area.

The statistical data for Israel are supplied by and under the responsibility of the relevant Israeli authorities. The use of such data by the OECD is without prejudice to the status of the Golan Heights, East Jerusalem and Israeli settlements in the West Bank under the terms of international law.

Please cite this publication as:
OECD (2022), *Delivering Quality Services to All in Alentejo: Preparing Regions for Demographic Change*, OECD Rural Studies, OECD Publishing, Paris, https://doi.org/10.1787/63ffb4d7-en.

ISBN 978-92-64-69173-5 (print)
ISBN 978-92-64-40664-3 (pdf)
ISBN 978-92-64-38668-6 (HTML)
ISBN 978-92-64-73515-6 (epub)

OECD Rural Studies
ISSN 2707-3416 (print)
ISSN 2707-3424 (online)

Foreword

Across and within OECD countries, significant gaps emerge in the access and quality of education and health services. Without action, shrinking and ageing populations in many rural communities are likely to experience rising unit costs due to population decline and increasing demand with higher shares of elderly, coupled with lower digital skill-levels and lower access to teachers and medical staff. These areas also suffer gaps in access to transport networks and digital connectivity, among many others. Hastened by the COVID-19 pandemic, there is now even greater urgency to embrace digital tools and adopt forward looking and effective policy levers to ensure the delivery of effective services to citizens living in rural communities.

This study focuses on education services in a multi-level governance context in the region of Alentejo (Portugal). It highlights the need for a better articulation and coordination among levels of government to improve the access and quality of education services. It also sheds light on the decisive role that geography plays and the importance of adopting a spatial lens to address the rising inequalities in access to education services in Portugal. The study provides guidance for Alentejo, represented by the Alentejo Regional Coordination and Development Commission CCDR-A (Comissão de Coordenação e Desenvolvimento Regional do Alentejo), and proposes sustainable and equitable long-term strategies for service delivery in the region. The national Cohesion and Development Agency (AD&C) also took part in and supported the elaboration of this study.

This study, which is part of the OECD workstream *Preparing Regions for Demographic Change*, was carried out as part of the OECD's Regional Development Policy Committee (RDPC) Programme of Work on OECD Rural Studies. The RDPC provides a unique forum for international exchange and debate on regional economies, policies and governance. It was discussed in the 26th meeting of the Working Party on Rural Policy and was approved by the RDPC [CFE/RDPC/RUR(2021)7] via written procedure on March 14, 2022.

Acknowledgements

This study was produced in the OECD Centre for Entrepreneurship, SMEs, Regions and Cities (CFE), led by Lamia Kamal-Chaoui, Director, as part of the programme of work of the Regional Development Policy Committee (RDPC).

The study was co-ordinated by Ana Isabel Moreno Monroy and Marc Bournisien de Valmont, under the supervision of Jose Enrique Garcilazo, Head of the Regional and Rural Policy Unit in the Regional Development and Multi-level Governance Division, led by Dorothée Allain-Dupré. The study was drafted by Ana Isabel Moreno Monroy and Marc Bournisien de Valmont (Chapters 2 and 4), and by Isidora Zapata and Antoine Kornprobst (Chapter 3). All authors contributed to Chapter 1.

The OECD is grateful to the Portuguese stakeholders, including the Alentejo Regional Coordination and Development Commission CCDR-A (António Ceia da Silva, Carmen Carvalheira, Joaquim Fialho, Teresa Godinho, and Carla Semêdo Lázaro), the Portuguese Cohesion and Development Agency (Nuno Oliveira Romão, Inacio Rui, and Catarina Portela) and OECD's RDPC Portuguese delegate Duarte Rodrigues. The OECD is also grateful to all stakeholders that contributed to the survey of the study and the mission. We are also grateful to the peer-reviewer Seonghee Min (Korea Research Institute for Human Settlements) for providing valuable inputs to the study. Special thanks are expressed to Isabelle Chatry, Varinia Michalun, Antti Moisio, Betty-Ann Bryce, and Philip Chan (CFE) who provided input in various stages. The OECD is also grateful to delegates of the Regional Development Policy Committee and its Working Party on Rural Policy for comments and guidance throughout the project.

Table of contents

Tables

Figures

Boxes

Follow OECD Publications on:

http://twitter.com/OECD_Pubs

http://www.facebook.com/OECDPublications

http://www.linkedin.com/groups/OECD-Publications-4645871

http://www.youtube.com/oecdilibrary

OECD Alerts http://www.oecd.org/oecddirect/

Executive summary

Alentejo, a sparsely-populated region in mid-south Portugal, has among the fastest decline in population and highest ageing rate across large OECD regions. This is expected to continue in the coming decades, putting pressure on local finances, which are already under severe strain because of the pandemic. The costs needed to provide good quality services in places with smaller and more dispersed populations are higher due to their smaller economies of scale and scope, higher transportation costs, and greater difficulties in attracting service professionals. Exacerbating this are important gaps in Alentejo's broadband infrastructure and digital skills, especially in its rural areas, creating bottlenecks for public authorities looking to deliver some public services digitally. Alentejo is not alone, many other OECD regions face similar challenges, and, like Alentejo, they will need to develop forward looking policy responses that can embrace the opportunities provided by digitalisation, as well as other innovative solutions, including through better coordination across levels of administration that can help overcome policy silos. Focusing on education, this study provides valuable lessons for regions and all levels of government experiencing decentralisation and facing demographic challenges.

Portugal's multi-level governance system is undergoing important structural changes in particular with the 2019 decentralisation framework that transfers additional responsibilities to municipalities. This transfer creates an opportunity for local governments to reorganise the provision of public services, such as school transport services, which recently became a municipal responsibility. However, these transfers have not always been accompanied by sufficient and adequate funding to handle the new responsibilities. In addition, in some cases, the transfers have resulted in inconsistencies. For example, while school closures remain a central government responsibility, municipalities now have to bear the higher students' travel costs related to the consolidation process. To enhance the ongoing decentralisation process it will be important to ensure that municipalities – not only in Alentejo but across Portugal – have sufficient and adequate resources to manage new tasks, avoiding underfunded mandates. In addition, better encouraging inter-municipal or inter-parish co-operation through fiscal incentives would allow Alentejo to better align service provision and local needs, enabling municipalities and parishes to find common solutions to the challenges brought by disperse, declining and ageing populations. This could help ensure that municipalities and inter-municipal bodies are able to properly and sustainably finance service provision and provide access to quality services. In parallel, to move forward with Portugal's regionalisation reforms, Alentejo could serve as a pilot experience of regional governance to foster territorial cohesion and regional development.

The provision of educational services in Alentejo is challenged by the national policy that closes and consolidates schools, coupled with the already long distances to schools. In sparsely populated areas, long travel distances can negatively affect student learning experiences and give rise to equity concerns. The consolidation policy particularly affects small rural municipalities and/or lagging regions with lower education quality, higher distances, and smaller school systems, and thus requires tailored strategies to ensure access to and good quality of education services. The simultaneous challenge of decreased demand for education services in the region as a whole, and the long-standing difficulties in attracting qualified teachers to rural areas, underscores the importance of nimble and adaptive policies. Downscaling the number of teachers in certain parts of the region, while at the same time making the rural regions more attractive as a place to live and work is not easy. As several teachers are deployed in rural areas by central decision-making rather than by choice, policies should encourage geographical mobility through incentives to help strengthen the quality of education in rural regions. The Alentejo region also needs to strengthen the use of digital infrastructure to bring opportunities to remote areas and improve the quality of services and lower their costs. Further digitalisation of public services – including the improvement of existing transport on demand IT services in Alentejo – and alternative solutions, such as encouraging student accommodation, might help to overcome school transportation challenges.

This study includes four chapters. Chapter 1 summarises the main assessments of the study and recommendations of Chapters 3 and 4 (listed in Table 1). Chapter 2 highlights the demographic and digital connectivity trends framing service delivery in Alentejo. Chapter 3 discusses multi-level governance and financing challenges for service provision in Alentejo. Finally, Chapter 4 analyses challenges to balance quality, cost and distance to education services in Alentejo.

Table 1. Key recommendations

Chapter	Recommendation	Who
Multi-level governance and subnational finance for service provision (Chapter 3)	Further pursuing decentralisation and regionalisation reforms to better align service provision and local need 1. Accompany the transfer of competences to municipalities with the transfer of sufficient and adequate financial resources to cover the administrative costs associated with the management of new tasks. 2. Pilot a new model of regional governance in Alentejo a way that coincides with NUTS2 to better align demographics trends with public services and better understand the differentiated needs of large and smaller municipalities.	National government, CCDR-A
	Strengthening cross-jurisdiction cooperation is necessary to make sure the planning and delivery of services are done at the right scale 3. Encourage IMCs through financial incentives by, for example, directing more transfers to IMCs, instead of to municipalities, particularly with respect to public services with important externalities. 4. Encourage peer-learning build on already successful IMCs mechanisms in the region (or in other regions in Portugal) and adopt a strategy to actively promote them. 5. Foster cooperation among parishes to enable them to effectively perform their tasks and deliver local services to residents. 6. Promote peer-learning experiences among regions that face similar challenges (i.e., shrinking and ageing population). 7. Identify municipalities or groups of municipalities pertaining to the same functional area that could benefit the most from scaling-up the provision of services.	National government, CCDR-A, Municipalities
	Adjusting fiscal arrangements to ensure municipalities can properly finance service provision and adapt to demographic trends 8. Strengthen the municipal own revenue base in a gradual manner, for example, by increasing the leverage that municipalities have on to tax rates (i.e. on the Property Tax and the Surcharge Tax), and the proportion of the personal income tax that stays with municipalities. 9. Guarantee financial means of IMCs to particularly benefit small municipalities that have less capacity to raise own revenues, for example, by increasing the amount of transfers to enlarge the role of IMCs	National government

Forward-looking planning for the provision of basic education (Chapter 4)	Taking into account the effects of demographic change is necessary to bridge the quality and access gaps and improve the restructuring and planning of the school network 10. Design a specific strategy to bridge quality and access gaps in lagging and remote rural municipalities 11. Use educational charters – a municipal strategic planning instrument aimed at reorganising the network of educational and pedagogical facilities – to coordinate actions among neighbouring municipalities 12. Encourage multi-level cooperation towards innovative models including service co-location, and plan strategically the location of new schools based on future demand projections	National government, CCDR-A, Municipalities
	Achieving better quality education also requires improving the geographic mobility of teachers while increasing within school efficiency 13. Revise the national model of teaching recruitment to include the participation of municipalities and regional authorities in the process 14. Enhance geographic mobility of teachers	National government
	Increased efforts are needed to bridge the digital divide and enhance the digitalisation of public services to overcome the challenges of school transport 15. Further develop transport on demand solutions 16. Increase cooperation between municipalities for the provision of transport 17. Create a committee of volunteer teachers at the regional level to support teachers from rural communities with the most difficulties in their adaptation and training process 18. Support networks bringing together employees from digital sectors and teachers	National government, CCDR-A, Municipalities, Inter-municipalities, School clusters
	Establishing a strategy for student accommodation could contribute to solve the challenges of school transport 19. Support the accommodation of students over 16 years of age during school days 20. Restructure the network of student residences in order to better match supply with demand efficiently	National government, CCDR-A, Municipalities

Note: The table includes the recommended timing for the implementation of each action and the level of government or organisations responsible for taking action.

Assessment and Recommendations

Demographic and digitalisation trends

1. Alentejo is experiencing one of the fastest rates of population decline and ageing across OECD regions

As in the rest of Portugal, Alentejo is experiencing population ageing and low in-migration due to the preference of nationals and migrants for coastal areas. Alentejo is Portugal's TL2 region with the highest share of elderly in the population (26% of +65) and lowest share of foreign-born population (4%). These forces, which have been gradually sustained over the past 50 years, have contributed to increase the ageing gap in Alentejo with respect to other Portuguese regions, and have contributed to economic and social decline in some municipalities. Indeed, more than half of the municipalities of the region have experienced sustained and strong population decline in recent decades. According to preliminary 2021 census data, Alentejo's population shrank at an annual rate of 0.72% on average between 2011 and 2021, four times faster than the national average (0.17%).

Moreover, projections from the Portuguese National Statistics Institute (INE) foresee a further 30% drop in Alentejo's population between 2020 and 2080. This trend will particularly affect the more remote areas of the region – which already have an elderly dependency ratio 10 percentage points higher than in other regions in Portugal. The four most remote TL3 regions in Alentejo are projected to shrink about three times faster in 2011-2035 (0.8% annually) compared to the TL3 region close to a small/medium city (0.27% annually). In addition, by 2035, only three municipalities are projected to grow, while 14 will sustain annual population decreases of 1% on average over 2011-2035.

These demographic developments have and will continue to lower the demand for education services in some areas and increase it for health care services. This will require adapting the provision of local public services in the region and building on efficiency gains across levels of government. Moreover, as demand recedes, municipal governments and parishes, mandated to provide equal access to all residents, will face higher costs from the lack of economies of scale and larger distances between settlements.

2. Broadband connectivity and digital gaps represent a major challenge for the provision of public services

Digital services present new opportunities for service delivery in remote areas where costs tend to be higher and quality lower. They can help to improve the quality and lower the cost of service delivery in these types of rural areas. The national government in Portugal has already undertaken several initiatives to strengthen digital services, including in education. Digital solutions can help address challenges in remote and low populated areas to deliver transport on demand services. Targeted actions can also help to reduce skills gaps of education professionals.

Despite recent efforts, broadband connectivity has not yet reached all corners of Alentejo, and rural inhabitants have less basic digital skills than urban inhabitants. According to broadband speed data[1] at the TL2 regional level, inhabitants in Alentejo experience, on average, speeds over 26% below the national average. Moreover, these gaps in broadband connection are compounded by the low level of digital skills.

According to national data for 2020, Portugal faces one of the lowest levels of basic or above digital skills in rural areas across the EU. Only 22% of Portuguese people living in rural areas have basic or above digital skills, compared to 60% in cities.

Multi-level governance and subnational finance

3. Further pursuing decentralisation and regionalisation reforms would allow Alentejo to better align service provision and local needs

The multi-level governance system in Portugal has been undergoing important structural changes in recent years, in particular with the 2019 framework for the transfers of new additional competencies to local authorities. The success of these reforms will depend, on how municipalities can maintain quality public service delivery in the face of a shrinking population and labour force, and the erosion of tax bases.

The transfer of competences from the central level to municipalities in particular regarding education, teaching and vocational training, as well as school transport has represented an opportunity for local governments, which have been able to reorganise, to a certain extent, the provision of public services. Decentralising tasks associated with school transport services, for example, facilitated the reorganisation of the network. In some cases, it also facilitated the closure of small schools and the reorganisation of the delivery of school transportation and education services in a more rational way with one school providing education services for different places.

The flip side is that the municipalities are struggling with finding a balance between the new decentralised competences and financing of their tasks. Central government transfers do not necessarily cover all the costs associated with the transfer of new competences, in particular, additional administrative costs that municipalities need to incur when dealing with new tasks, including adjustments in functions in order to deliver new tasks and new, often onerous, administrative procedures. In addition, in some cases, the transfers have resulted in inconsistencies. For example, while school closures remain a central government responsibility, municipalities now have to bear the higher costs of students' travel reflecting the consolidation process. Some key avenues to further enhance regionalisation and decentralisation reforms and ensure these reforms meet its objectives, are as follows:

- **Recommendation 1** – The transfer of competences to municipalities needs to be accompanied with the transfer of sufficient and adequate financial resources to cover the administrative costs associated with the management of new tasks. To encourage municipalities to take over more responsibilities in the context of the decentralisation reform, municipalities should receive more fiscal resources (from grants) and powers (more own-source revenues) aligned with the new tasks that would be assigned (see below). Beyond the transfer of resources it is important to ensure that municipalities have adequate human resources and necessary tools (e.g. IT tools) to undertake the new tasks that have been assigned.

- **Recommendation 2** – Alentejo could serve as a pilot to experiment a new model of regional governance to be consistent with NUTS2 definition and better align demographics trends with public services and better understand the differentiated needs of large and smaller municipalities. Different options are available. Co-operative regionalisation can be seen as an alternative to full regionalisation but also as an intermediate stage towards full regionalisation.

4. Strengthening cross-jurisdiction cooperation is necessary to make sure the planning and delivery of services are done at the right scale

The lack of an intermediate regional level in Portugal affects the efficient provision of services in Alentejo as the central government might be too large and municipalities too small to deliver services effectively. At the same time, municipal mergers are not necessarily an efficient solution as municipalities are already large and not densely populated. In this context, the role played by the Alentejo Regional Coordination and Development Commission (CCDR-A) has been crucial in ensuring a whole-of-region approach to service delivery challenges. The CCDR facilitates a mutual understanding among municipalities and inter-municipal communities (IMCs) to find a regional-level framework that better takes into account challenges identified by IMCs in their strategies. Still, while the CCDR-A helps in bringing clarity and enabling co-ordination at the regional level, it only covers four sub-regions – Lezíria do Tejo, which for statistical purposes pertain to the TL2 regional definition, and for administrative purposes is part of the Lisbon region. It has also proven difficult to coordinate sectoral, territorial, and regional policies in Alentejo as the multiplicity of sectoral actors at different levels of government makes co-ordination challenging.

The creation of IMCs and the gradual transfer of competences to municipalities has supported horizontal coordination, municipalities and parishes in Alentejo. IMCs in Alentejo, as is the case in other Portuguese regions, have effectively enabled municipal cooperation in various strategic areas where local service delivery may benefit from increasing scale and improved inter-governmental coordination. IMCs conduct projects that are key to promote regional development such as inter-municipal climate change adaptation, mapping social, health and educational services within its territory, or the co-ordination of vocational programmes.

Nonetheless, the current Portuguese multi-level governance framework does not facilitate the delivery of services with region-wide benefits, such as healthcare or transport – the latter being provided at the IMC level in Alentejo. IMCs do not necessarily cover the appropriate scale for regional development policies. Moreover, in some cases, it has been difficult to stimulate participation of municipalities in IMC projects as they do not necessarily see the advantages of supra-municipal coordination. In addition, since decision making by IMCs requires unanimity among municipalities, the line of actions and investment by IMCs remains limited.

Further encouraging inter-municipal association to provide decentralised services could improve service provision in education, health care and social support. The central government needs to adopt a proactive role in promoting and stimulating inter-municipal cooperation in the provision of decentralised services. For this, the following actions could be beneficial:

- **Recommendation 3** – The central government could encourage IMCs through financial incentives that foster cooperation across jurisdictions. One way to accomplish this could be directing more transfers to IMCs, instead of to municipalities, particularly with respect to public services with important externalities.

- **Recommendation 4** – Encourage peer-learning building on already successful inter-municipal co-operation mechanisms in the region (and in other regions in Portugal) and adopt a strategy to actively promote them.

- **Recommendation 5** – Foster cooperation among parishes to enable them to effectively perform their tasks and deliver local services to residents. In some cases, parishes would benefit from cooperating with adjacent parishes in another municipality.

- **Recommendation 6** – Promote peer-learning experiences explore instances of co-operation with neighbouring regions and knowledge sharing with regions that face similar challenges (i.e., shrinking and ageing population). This peer learning, while promoted by the central level, could, for example, be conducted with regions in Spain that are currently facing similar challenges.

- **Recommendation 7** – Identify municipalities or groups of municipalities pertaining to the same functional area that could benefit the most from scaling-up the provision of services. This mapping needs to identify which services may benefit from joint-provision considering functional areas, and not necessarily the administrative divisions of IMCs currently in place.

5. Adjusting fiscal arrangements to ensure municipalities can properly finance service provision and adapt to demographic trends

The ageing and shrinking of Alentejo's population affects: (i) the type of services that local governments need to finance, and (ii) local government capacity to finance the provision of services. The ongoing change of Alentejo's demographic structure will have a strong impact on education, health and long-term care services, but also on public infrastructure. Given the ageing trend, it is expected that public spending on age-related programs will increase. At the same time, the declining population is likely to have a negative effect on economic activity, resulting in a slowdown in public revenue growth. Shrinking population also means shrinking municipal tax bases. This represents an important challenge for services financing in Alentejo, where direct and shared taxes revenue account for a large share of total subnational government's revenue. Given the design of the transfer system, declining population also means a reduction of the transfers received from the central level.

While the fiscal framework for local authorities has undergone reforms in recent years (2007, 2013, 2018) to strengthen municipal finance and improve its sustainability, the fiscal situation of municipalities in Alentejo is still challenging. First, the transition from a centrally financed model to a model which is based on greater self-reliance at the subnational government level has been slow. Second, while direct and shared tax revenues represent a significant share of municipal revenues, municipal tax bases in Alentejo tend to be below the national average. Third, central government transfers to municipalities, in particular capital transfers, have decreased since 2010, as a result of national fiscal consolidation measures. Finally, an ageing and shrinking population put at stake the current funding models of local public services in the region.

IMCs have only a restricted capacity to raise own revenues and are mainly financed by municipalities. The limited financial means of these entities puts pressure on their capacity to be effective service providers and may restrict the incentive of municipalities to utilise the IMCs.

Current fiscal arrangements in Portugal do not always take into account territorial, social and economic specificities, and, ultimately, the changing needs of each territory resulting from demographic changes. This means that many municipalities in Alentejo especially those that are smaller and scarcely populated –and which are ultimately the most affected by the demographic challenge-, face large difficulties in providing access to quality services in a sustainable way. Fiscal arrangements need to be gradually reformed in order to ensure that municipalities will still be able to properly finance service provision and ensure citizen's well-being over time. For this, some of the measures that could be taken are the following:

- **Recommendation 8** – Strengthen the municipal own revenue base in a gradual manner. A high reliance on transfers and a low taxing power may have a negative effect on the efficiency of municipal service delivery. This can be done by increasing the leverage that municipalities have on tax rates (i.e. on the Property Tax and the Surcharge Tax), and the proportion of the personal income tax that stays with municipalities.

- **Recommendation 9** – Guarantee financial means of IMCs to particularly benefit small municipalities that have less capacity to raise own revenues. It would be important to increase the amount of transfers to enlarge the role of IMCs and make them less dependent on the municipal will of delegating task. The increase of transfers for IMCs can be subject to particular results or outputs that should be previously defined and agreed between the central level and the concerned IMCs.

6. Taking into account the effects of demographic change is necessary to bridge the quality and access gaps and improve the restructuring and planning of the school network

The 2005 school consolidation reform in Portugal – addressing the school network's inefficiency and strong regional inequalities – accomplished the goal of reducing the number of redundant schools, especially in rural areas. Between 2005 and 2010, school consolidation in Portugal proceeded based on a fixed threshold of students per school but that did not take into account the effect of geography and demography on rural schools. These thresholds have since been removed and replaced by a policy of case-by-case evaluation between the national government and municipalities. However, more needs to be done, the costs of school consolidation should be fully accounted for when weighing the efficiency benefits of school consolidation. At present, there is no accounting of the full costs of consolidation including not only direct transport costs, but also indirect costs linked to long travel distances, such as the societal costs when a student dropouts. Given the fast progression of school consolidation and the already long distances to schools many students face, the national government should pay special attention to designing tailored strategies for small rural municipalities and lagging regions that have failed to improve education quality and that have high distances and small schools.

Moreover, municipalities need further flexibility to adapt to the effects of demographic change on the school network. Under the second generation of educational charters – a municipal strategic planning instrument aimed at reorganising the network of educational and pedagogical facilities – some municipalities have built their own municipal principles in order to align the reorganisation of the school network with the educational policy defined at the local level.

In order to bridge the quality and access gaps in education and improve the restructuring and planning of the school network, the following actions could be beneficial:

- **Recommendation 10** – Design a specific strategy to bridge quality and access gaps in lagging and remote rural municipalities. The national government should undertake cost-benefit analyses that fully take into account the effect of school closures on the accessibility of students living in the most remote areas and associated costs of school transport. It should also commission a dedicated study projecting the financial sustainability of the current model given demographic projections, taking into account structural under-investment in physical infrastructure in these areas as well as the regional context.
- **Recommendation 11** – Use educational charters to coordinate actions among neighbouring municipalities. In the framework of increased planning at the level of inter-municipal communities (IMCs), the creation of inter-municipal school network planning instruments, such as inter-municipal education charters, would allow planning beyond municipal administrative boundaries as well as a better comprehension of the different needs of rural areas within the region.
- **Recommendation 12** – The national government should work closely with municipalities and regional authorities towards innovative models including service co-location, and plan strategically the location of new schools based on future demand projections.

7. Achieving better quality education also requires improving the geographic mobility of teachers while increasing within school efficiency

As demonstrated in the current study, increasing within school efficiency can lead to substantial cost-savings. Student-to-teacher ratios in Alentejo and Portugal remain small by international standards, so the focus could be on finding mechanisms to continue increasing within school efficiency while maintaining similar quality levels, for instance by reconsidering the spread of the vocational offer in upper secondary schools and investing in small and multi-grade classroom teaching skills. While the geographic and demographic conditions in some rural areas imply a lower achievable student-to-teacher ratio, this could lead to substantial savings in towns and suburbs.

More generally, like other countries experiencing population decline and ageing, Portugal needs to downscale on the number of teachers to keep in line with decreased demand for education services, while also focusing on rebalancing higher demand in urban areas and lower demand in rural areas. The process of downscaling proceeds in a context of ageing of a substantial part of the teaching staff, and increasing difficulties in attracting teachers to rural areas, especially those that require long travel times. However, the ability of Alentejo to design tailored solutions for teacher shortages issues is limited given that teaching responsibilities remain under the full control of the national government. Currently, the deployment of teachers in rural areas is mainly a result of centralised decisions rather than personal choices. The impact of recruitment policies can affect teacher motivation and increase rural-urban gaps in the quality of education. The national government could consider the following actions to improve the geographical mobility of teachers while increasing within school efficiency:

- **Recommendation 13** – Revise the national model of teaching recruitment to include the participation of municipalities and regional authorities in the process. This would better align needs and motivation of teachers and would help considering retention strategies for teachers in order to reduce the high turnover in rural schools.

- **Recommendation 14** – Geographic mobility of teachers – especially young ones – could be enhanced with career incentives, experience-sharing networks by more experienced teachers, and more clear compensation for long travel times that go beyond financial compensation (e.g. flexible work hours, shorter dedication in classrooms, rotation systems for itinerant teachers, accommodation support).

8. Increased efforts are needed to bridge the digital divide and enhance the digitalisation of public services to overcome the challenges of school transport

The balance between costs, access and quality is currently fragmented across levels of government: municipalities assume the transportation costs that in a large part result from consolidation while the national government manages the school network. This model is prone to lead to higher spatial inequalities, as remote and small rural municipalities find themselves under pressure on all fronts – cost, distance and quality – while also having lower capacity to deal with a complex and costly organisation of transportation services. Therefore, school transportation is one of the main concerns of Alentejo rural inhabitants as long travel distances and significant time of travel negatively affect students' learning experience and represent a significant educational equity problem.

In this context, digitalisation provides a powerful way to overcome the trade-offs between cost efficiency and access. Regarding education, Portugal has recently made substantial progress in its strategy for digital education and has started exploring transport on demand services, which can be a solution against the alternative of increasing the time frequencies of the traditional transport system, in a scenario where both would lead to increased access and decreased travel times for students. The benefits of transport on demand and digital education are however greatly limited by the digital divide in Alentejo. Internet connection is more limited in Alentejo and rural areas than in other regions and urban areas and rural inhabitants have lower basic digital skills than urban inhabitants.

It is essential to reduce digital gaps in rural areas in order to set up efficient transport on demand services. Assisting rural communities to bridge broadband access and uptake gaps is critical to improve their quality of life and their access to Internet-based digital services. In the framework of the European Recovery Funds, Portugal's plan allocates 22% of the funds to measures in favour of the digital transition (European Commission, 2021[1]). Part of the funds should enable greater investment in broadband infrastructure in rural and sparsely populated areas of Portugal with the largest connectivity gaps, such as Alentejo, and in particular, the sub-regions of Alentejo Central and Baixo Alentejo. This effort will strongly contribute to reduce the existing gap in access to public services in rural areas.

In order to tackle the challenge of school transportation and digital skills gaps in rural areas, the study suggests the following actions:

- **Recommendation 15** – Further develop transport on demand solutions. Alentejo authorities should develop further the current *Transporte a pedido*"[2] service in the near future and make it more dynamic. By incorporating a more sophisticated software, the service could provide users with reliable and comprehensive real-time information, the possibility to make last-minute bookings from a mobile application or by phone, and the adaptation of routes, stops and schedules to users demand. Transport on demand services benefit the entire rural population, from dependent people needing access to basic services, to teachers and upper secondary and vocational students – with more flexible schedules – living in remote areas.

- **Recommendation 16** – Increase cooperation between municipalities for the provision of transport. A supra-municipal perspective and greater cooperation between municipalities, inter-municipalities and school clusters could be beneficial for school transport in Alentejo. This would allow better integration of transport on demand services with regional and national bus networks as well as scaling services from a local to a regional level. Regional transport partnerships across the Alentejo region and further spaces for dialogue between local stakeholders to improve school transport should be encouraged.

- **Recommendation 17** – Create a committee of volunteer teachers at the regional level to support teachers from rural communities with the most difficulties in their adaptation and training process. This would help to ensure that the target of 100% of teachers with digital capabilities by 2023 is achieved specifically in rural areas.

- **Recommendation 18** – Alentejo regional authorities should support networks bringing together employees from digital sectors and teachers in order to review and improve the new ICT curriculum guidelines as well as to better inform students on the broad opportunities offered by digital careers and the digital skills required to access them.

9. Establishing a strategy for student accommodation could contribute to solve the challenges of school transport

The few existing student residences in Alentejo are managed by municipalities and supported by national administration funds or will soon be according to the decentralisation programme (Decree-Law no. 21/2019). Student accommodation can be an effective alternative to tackle school transport issues and to avoid that, due to poor access in rural areas, many students are limited to choosing educational programmes that are closer to where they live. On the other hand, due to a mismatch between supply and demand, some of the student residences provided by the Ministry of Education throughout the country are not operational due to a lack of demand. The actions identified on these issues include:

- **Recommendation 19** – Support the accommodation of students over 16 years of age – as they have more flexible timetables that are difficult to accommodate with a regular transport system – during school days. In the framework of multi-level cooperation, this action could contribute to avoiding daily transport problems – and consequently study performance related issues – as well as to allow young people in Alentejo to have a wider educational offer and thus more career opportunities. European Recovery Funds could finance all or part of these residences.

Recommendation 20 – Implement a national plan to restructure the network of student residences in order to better match supply with demand efficiently and to concentrate student residences where they are most needed.

References

European Commission (2021), *NextGenerationEU: European Commission endorses Portugal's €16.6 billion recovery and resilience plan*, Press release, 16 June 2021, Brussels, https://ec.europa.eu/commission/presscorner/detail/en/ip_21_2985. [1]

Notes

[1] Data from self-administered speed tests by Ookla is presented as deviations from the national average to highlight within-country differences in the quality of broadband connections.

[2] Alentejo launched in 2019 the pilot transport on demand project "*Transporte a pedido*". It has 25 circuits in Baixo Alentejo (Beja, Mértola, Moura), Alentejo Litoral (Odemira) and Alentejo Central (Reguengos de Monsaraz).

2 Demographic and digitalisation trends

Introduction

The region of Alentejo is one of Portugal's seven TL2 regions. The region has five inter-municipal communities (CIM) and 58 municipalities, including its main city, Évora (Alentejo Central). The region borders Extremadura and Andalucía (Spain) on the East, the Atlantic Ocean and Metropolitan Area of: Lisbon on the West, Algarve in the South and Centro Region in the North. With 704 934 inhabitants, Alentejo is the fourth Portuguese TL2 region in terms of population. With 31 605 km² corresponding to about one third of the national surface, Alentejo is the largest Portuguese TL2 region in terms of surface. The population density of Alentejo (23 inhabitants per km²) is five times lower than the national level (113 inhabitants per km²) and is the lowest across Portugal's TL2 regions (Table 2.1).

This chapter outlines the main demographic trends framing service provision in Alentejo at the large region (TL2), small region (TL3) and degree of urbanisation levels. This last typology classifies settlements into sparse rural areas, villages, towns and suburbs and cities in an internationally comparable way (see Annex A for more details). The chapter starts by outlining the distribution of population across regions and human settlement types. In the second section, it analyses available population projections at different levels of territorial aggregation. In the third and last section, it gives an overview of digital divides across regions and degrees of urbanisation.

Population distribution and demographic trends

Alentejo has five TL3 regions, including one non-metropolitan region close to a small/medium city (Lezíria do Tejo, comprising 33.5% of the population) and four remote regions (Alentejo Central (where Évora is located), 21.6%; Alentejo Litoral, 13.6%; Baixo Alentejo, 16.3% and Alto Alentejo, 14.9%) (Figure 2.1). By degree of urbanisation, the population of the region is split rather evenly between towns and suburbs (39%), villages (32%) and sparse rural areas (29%) (Table 2.1). Meanwhile, Portugal has a smaller share of population in villages (9%) and sparse rural areas (23%), and most of the population concentrated in towns and suburbs (35%) and cities (33%). Unlike most OECD TL3 regions, Alentejo does not have any urban clusters that fall under the "cities" category.

Population size varies widely across the 58 municipalities in Alentejo. According to the preliminary results from the latest census, in 2021 population levels ranged from 1 435 inhabitants in Barrancos (Baixo Alentejo) (also the least populated municipality in Portugal mainland) to 58 770 inhabitants in Santarém (Lezíria do Tejo). In 2021, 16 out of 58 municipalities (28%) had 5 000 inhabitants or less, a higher share compared to 47 out of 308 (15%) at the national level.

Figure 2.1. Typology of regions and human settlements in Alentejo (NUTS3)

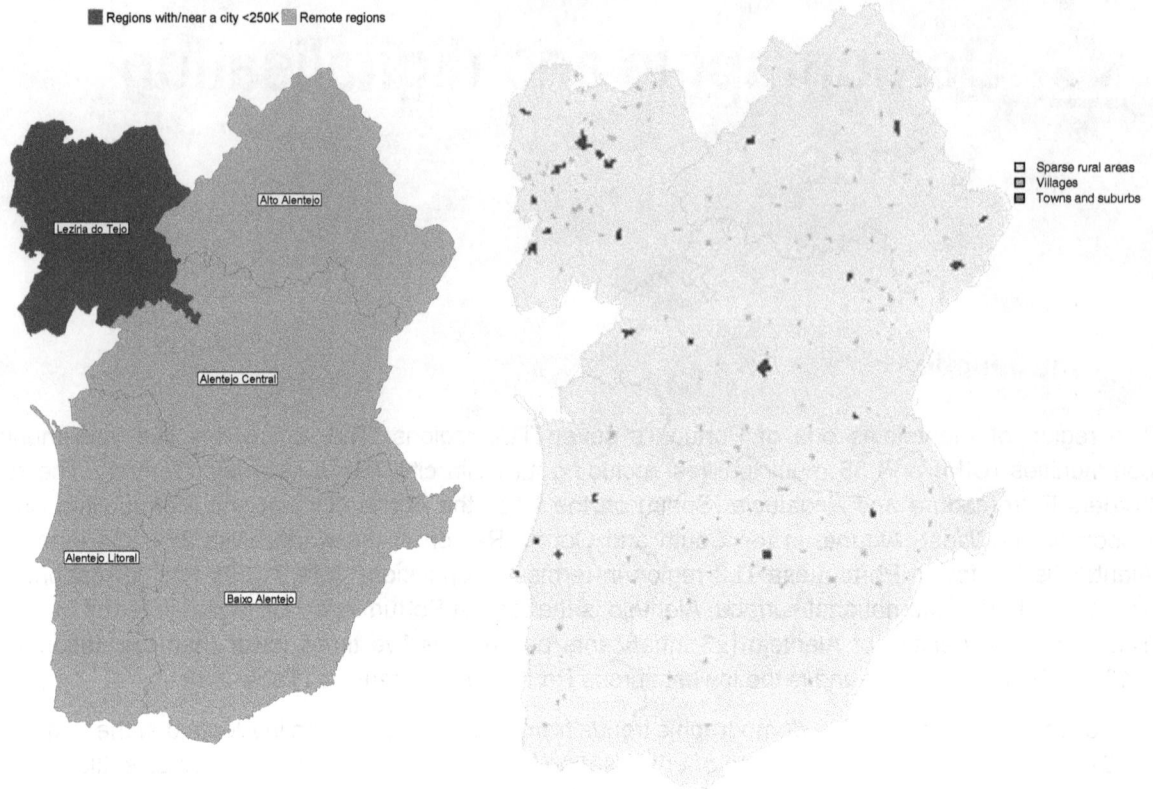

Note: See Annex A for a definition of degree of urbanisation areas.
Source: Authors' elaboration based on the GHSL database (accessed on May 2021).

According to the preliminary 2021 census data, Alentejo's population shrank at a rate of 0.72% annually between 2011 and 2021, four times faster than the national average (0.17%) (Table 2.1). While all Portuguese TL2 regions, except Lisbon Metropolitan Area and Algarve, experienced population decline in the last decade, Alentejo's population decline was the fastest across regions, followed by R.A da Madeira (0.4%) and Centro (0.44%). Four municipalities in Alentejo where among the top 10 municipalities in Portugal in terms of population decline (Barrancos, 1st , Nisa 4th , Gavião, 7th and Mora, 9th).

As in the rest of Portugal, a decreasing share of young people, an increasing share of the elderly and low in-migration drive depopulation in Alentejo. Alentejo is the Portuguese TL2 region with the highest share of elderly, with over one-quarter (26%) of the population above 65 years old (3.4 percentage points above the national level). Alentejo is also the peninsular Portuguese TL2 region with the lowest share of foreign-born population (4%).

Table 2.1. Summary of demographic indicators

	Pop. Density (per km²) (2020)	Annual % Pop. Growth (2011-2021)	Share of Elderly (65+) in total Pop. (%) (2020)	Share of Foreign-born Pop. (%) (2015)
Alentejo	22.1	-0.72	25.6	4.0
Portugal	111.7	-.0.17	22.2	6.8
OECD	38.4	0.51	13.1	10.0

Note: The OECD share of elderly calculations is based on 2019 values and the annual population growth rate on 2011-2020 values. The share of foreign-born population for OECD is an average of the values of 295 TL2 regions in 27 OECD countries.
Source: (OECD, 2021[1]) and (Statistics Portugal, 2021[2])

In Alentejo, a handful of municipalities with good access to Lisbon and Algarve have been gaining population in the last five decades, while more than half of the municipalities of the region have faced sustained and strong population decline. In 1960-2011, population growth ranged from -2.4% annually in Mértola (Baixo Alentejo) to 1.78% in Benavente, a municipality from the Lezíria do Tejo region located close to Lisbon. In fact, in the period 1960-2011 only 9 out of 58 municipalities, mostly located near Lisbon, registered positive population growth. Meanwhile, 29 municipalities sustained population decrease of at least 1% annually, and 6 municipalities including Mértola, Odemira (Alentejo Litoral), Serpa and Moura (Baixo Alentejo), Montemor-o-Novo (Alentejo Central) and Nisa (Alto Alentejo) lost at least 10 thousand inhabitants in those five decades.

Recent data from the 2021 Census at the Parish level further clarifies the spillover effect of Portugal's growing regions (Algarve and Lisbon Metropolitan Area) on Alentejo's settlement trends. In 2021, 20% of Parishes (65 out of 324) experienced population decreases of at least 2% annually (Figure 2.2). These Parishes concentrated in inland and Central areas of the region. Meanwhile, only 8% of Parishes (27) showed population growth. The parishes that grew or maintained population in the last decade where mostly located in Coastal areas and near Lisbon Metropolitan Region and Algarve.

Figure 2.2. Population change in Alentejo, by parishes

2011-2021

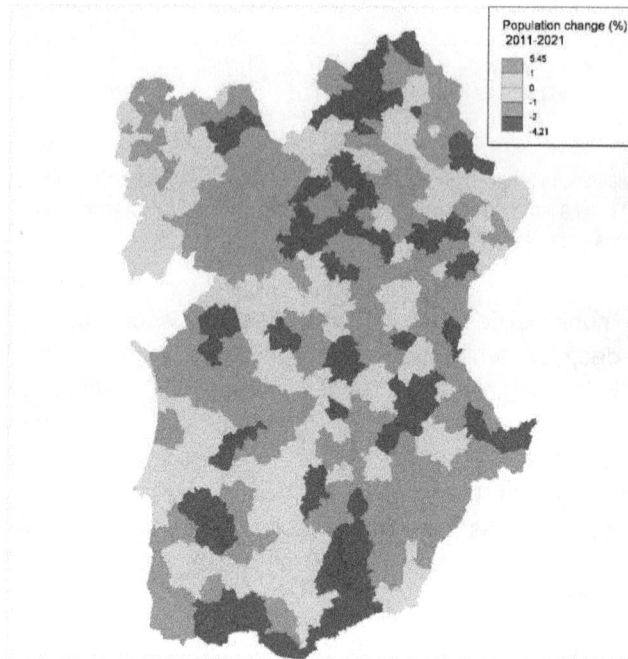

Note: Population change calculated as annual growth rate.
Source: (Statistics Portugal, 2021[2]) and (Agência para a Modernização Administrativa, 2021[3]) for the boundaries.

Future population projections

According to the Resident Population Projections 2020-2080 of the Portuguese National Statistics Institute (INE), the population of Alentejo could fall by almost 30% between 2020 and 2080, from around 704 000 inhabitants to around 495 000 inhabitants (INE, 2020[4]). In this scenario, the young population (0-14 years) of Alentejo would fall by 33% and the older population (65 years and over) would grow by around 4.4%.

Figure 2.3. Population projection, Alentejo, 2020-2080

By age groups

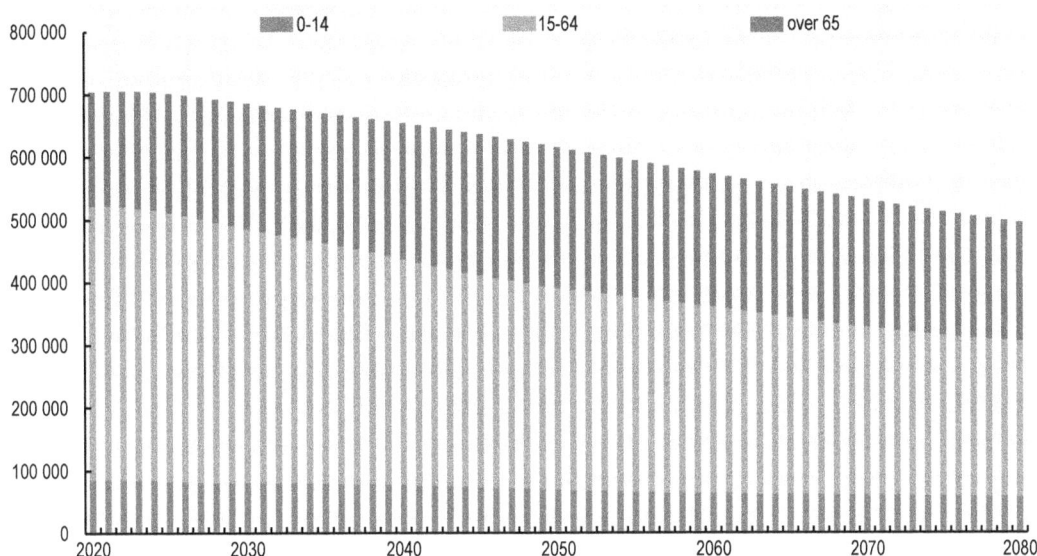

Note: Resident population in Alentejo tends to decrease until 2080 in any of the projected scenarios. The results presented are based on the central scenario of evolution for resident population. In terms of fertility, this scenario expects a moderate recovery of future fertility levels until 2080, with the Total Fertility Rate (TFR) reaching 1.59 children per woman in 2080. In terms of mortality, the gains in life expectancy observed over the last recent years are expected to persist, with life expectancy at birth reaching 87.92 years for men and 93.30 years for women in 2080. In terms of international migrations, trends in immigration and emigration are expected to continue in this central scenario, with the maintenance of positive annual international net migration over the projection period, reaching a net migration of 14 020 in 2080 (11 570 in 2018).
Source: (INE, 2020[4]), Resident population projections 2018-2080, 31 March 2020, https://www.ine.pt/xportal/xmain?xpid=INE&xpgid=ine_destaques&DESTAQUESdest_boui=406534255&DESTAQUESmodo=2.

Population shrinking and ageing will be a particular challenge in remote regions, which already have an elderly dependency ratio 10 percentage points higher than in other types of regions in Portugal (OECD, 2020[5]). The four remote TL3 regions in Alentejo are projected to shrink about three times faster in 2011-2035 (0.8% annually) compared to the TL3 region close to a small/medium city (0.27% annually), in line with national trends (0.89% versus 0.2%).

Furthermore, Alentejo is projected to have a significantly higher proportion of dependent-to-working persons over a 40-year horizon. The dependency rate is projected to increase from 6 dependent persons for every 10 working-age persons in 2020 to above 9 dependent persons for every 10 working-age persons after 2045. This dependency rate is comparable to Norte and Centro regions but is considerably above Lisbon, Algarve, R.A. Açores and R.A. Madeira (Figure 2.4).

Figure 2.4. Projected dependency ratios, Portugal, TL2 regions, 2020-2060

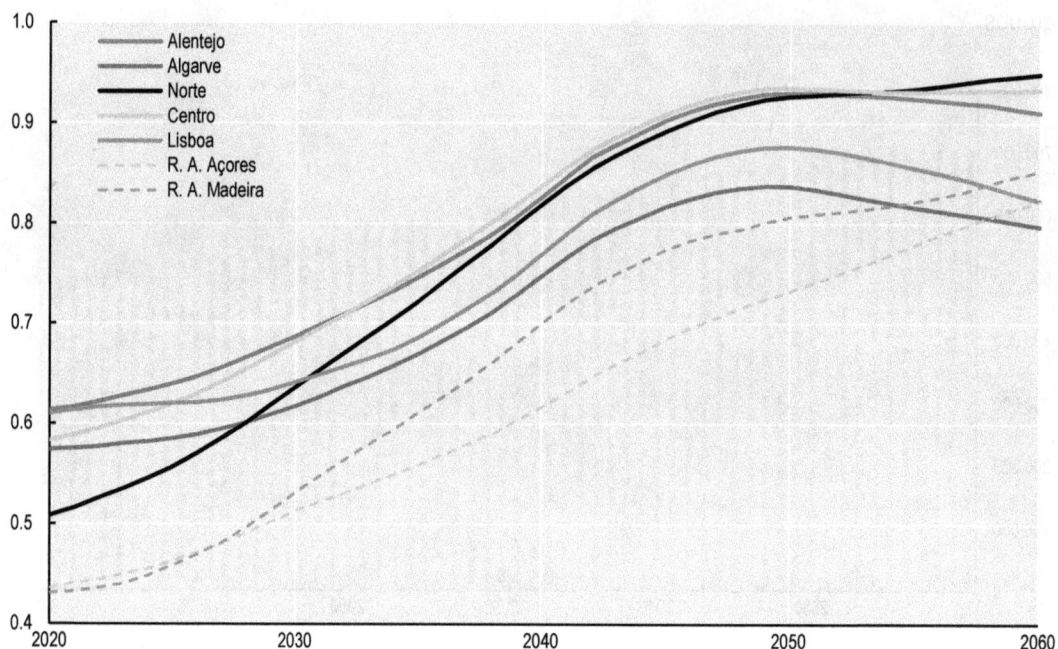

Note: The dependency ratio is the ratio between the total population aged 0-14 inclusive and 65+ inclusive over the total population aged between 14 and 65 exclusive.
Source: (INE, 2014[6]) Resident population projections 2012-2060, 28 March 2014, http://www.ine.pt/ngt_server/attachfileu.jsp?look_parentBoui=215593961&att_display=n&att_download=y.

By 2035, only three municipalities are projected to grow, while 14 municipalities will sustain population decreases of 1% annually over 2011-2035, with the largest decreases expected in Alandroal (Alentejo Central) (2.57% annually), Vendas Novas (Alentejo Central) (1.79%) and Nisa (1.78%). Compared to 1960, only a few small municipalities mostly located in Lezíria do Tejo are expected to have higher population in 2035, while all the largest municipalities including Santarém and Évora and all the municipalities of Baixo Alentejo are expected to be smaller in 2035 compared to 1960 (Figure 2.5).

Figure 2.5. Population in 1960 versus projected population in 2035 by municipality

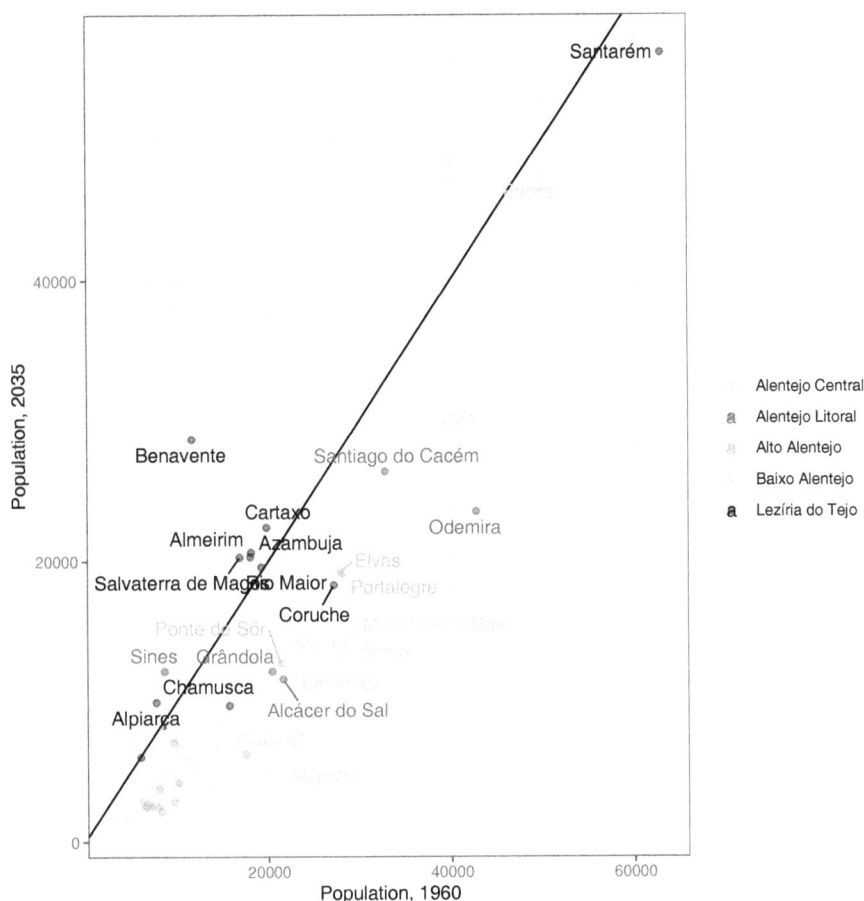

Source: Authors' elaboration based on (Goujon A., Jacobs-Crisioni C., Natale F., Lavalle C. (Eds), 2021[7]) and (Jacobs-Crisioni, C., C. Perpiña Castillo, J.-P. Aurambout, C. Lavalle, C. Baranzelli, and F. Batista e Silva, (nd)[8]).

Across degrees of urbanisation, towns and suburbs are projected to shrink faster than other areas between 2011 and 2035 (0.7% annually versus 0.6% in villages and 0.5% in sparse rural areas). Given that towns and suburbs have the highest initial birth rates and the lowest initial death rates across categories (Table 2.2), the faster rate of decline may be due to higher out-migration of working-age people compared to other areas.

Table 2.2. Summary of demographic indicators by degree of urbanisation, Alentejo 2011-2035

Degree of urbanisation	Population 2011	Share 2011	Population 2035	Share 2035	Annual pop. Growth 2011-2035	Birth rate 2011	Birth rate 2035	Death Rate 2011	Death Rate 2035
Sparse rural	220 292	29%	194 224	30%	-0.5	6.5	6.7	16.0	16.1
Villages	243 241	32%	212 748	33%	-0.6	6.7	6.7	15.8	15.5
Towns and suburbs	291 189	39%	243 627	37%	-0.7	7.7	7.3	11.5	13.0
Total	754 722		650 600						

Note: Death rates per 100 thousand inhabitants. Annual growth is calculated using compound growth rates.
Source: Authors' elaboration based on (Goujon A., Jacobs-Crisioni C., Natale F., Lavalle C. (Eds), 2021[7]) and (Jacobs-Crisioni, C., C. Perpiña Castillo, J.-P. Aurambout, C. Lavalle, C. Baranzelli, and F. Batista e Silva, (nd)[8]).

Digital divides

Speed broadband data[1] at the TL2 regional level shows that inhabitants in Alentejo experience, on average, speeds that are over 26% below the national average (Figure 2.6). In contrast, inhabitants of Lisbon's metropolitan area experience, on average, fixed download speeds that are over 17% above the national average. Across Portuguese TL2 regions, the digital gap in Alentejo is only surpassed by the Algarve region, with speeds that are over 40% below the national average.

Download speeds also differ across TL3 regions within Alentejo: while inhabitants of Alto Alentejo and Lezíria do Tejo experience, on average, fixed download speeds that are 22% and 23% below the national average, inhabitants in Baixo Alentejo and Alentejo Central experience, on average, speeds that are over 30% below the national average (Figure 2.6).

Figure 2.6. Gaps in download speeds experienced by users in Portugal TL2 regions and Alentejo TL3 regions

Ookla tests on fixed download speed, gaps estimated as percentage deviation from national averages (2020Q4)

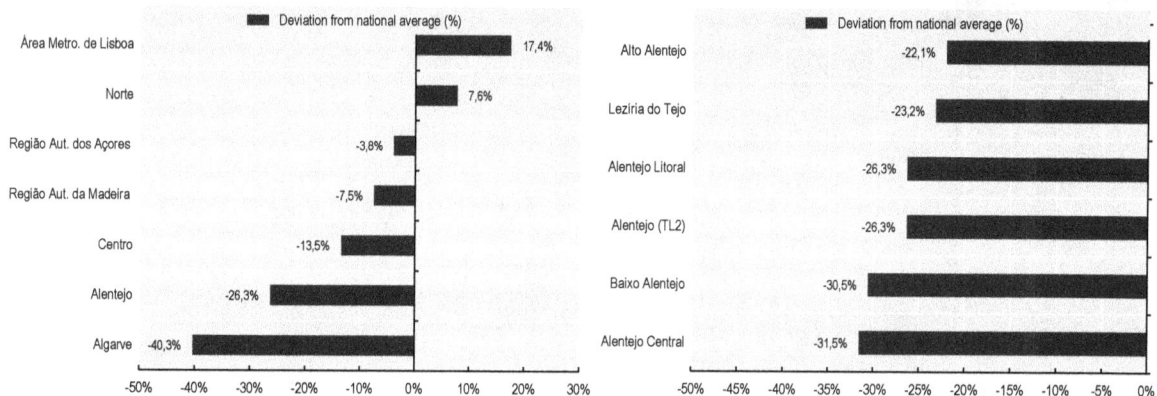

Note: Speedtest data corresponds to 2020Q4. The data for average fixed broadband download Speedtests reported by Ookla measures the sustained peak throughput achieved by users of the network. Measurements are based on self-administered tests by users, carried over iOS and mobile devices. The figure presents average peak speed tests, weighted by the number of tests.
Source: OECD calculations based on Speedtest® by Ookla® Global Fixed and Mobile Network Performance Maps. Based on analysis by Ookla of Speedtest Intelligence® data for 2020Q4. Provided by Ookla and accessed 2021-01-27. Ookla trademarks used under license and reprinted with permission.

Moreover, people living outside urban areas in Alentejo – especially those living in Alentejo Central – experience, on average, worse connection speeds. In Alentejo, while people living in towns and suburbs experience speeds that are close to the national average (3% below), rural inhabitants experience much slower speeds than the national average (42% below) (Figure 2.7). While residents of towns and suburbs in Alentejo Litoral experience speeds that are over 8% the national average, residents of rural areas in Alentejo Central experience download speeds 44% below the national average. In comparison, national level rural-urban gaps go in the same direction but are smaller (32% below).

Figure 2.7. Gaps in download speeds experienced by users in Portugal and Alentejo by degree of urbanisation

Ookla tests on fixed download speed, gaps estimated as percentage deviation from national averages (2020Q4)

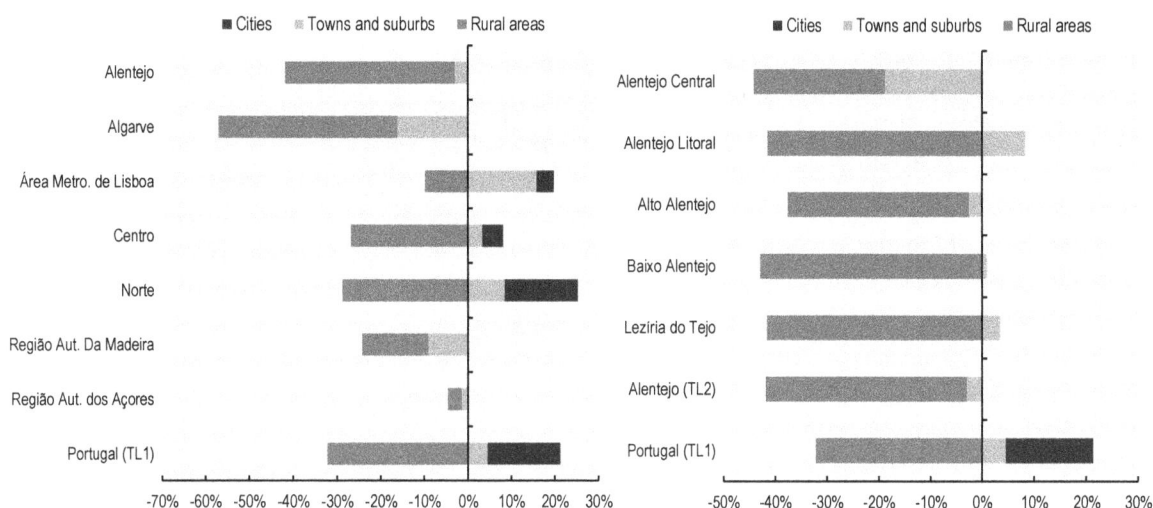

Note: Speedtest data corresponds to 2020Q4. The data for average fixed broadband download Speedtests reported by Ookla measures the sustained peak throughput achieved by users of the network. Measurements are based on self-administered tests by users, carried over iOS and mobile devices. Aggregation according to the degree of urbanisation was based on GHS Settlement Model (GHS-SMOD) layer grids. The figure presents average peak speed tests, weighted by the number of tests.
Source: OECD calculations based on Speedtest® by Ookla® Global Fixed and Mobile Network Performance Maps. Based on analysis by Ookla of Speedtest Intelligence® data for 2020Q4. Provided by Ookla and accessed 2021-01-27. Ookla trademarks used under license and reprinted with permission.

Data on digital skills gap is unfortunately not available at the regional level. Available data at the national level for 2020 reveals that only 22% of people living in rural areas in Portugal have basic or above digital skills, compared to 60% in cities (OECD, 2021[9]). However, Portugal's rural-urban gap in digital skills aligns with EU levels.

References

Agência para a Modernização Administrativa (2021), "Portal de dados abertos da Administração Pública", *Freguesias de Portugal*, https://dados.gov.pt/en/datasets/freguesias-de-portugal/ (accessed on 22 September 2021). [3]

Goujon A., Jacobs-Crisioni C., Natale F., Lavalle C. (Eds) (2021), *The demographic landscape of EU territories: challenges and opportunities in diversely ageing regions*, EUR 30498 EN, Publications Office of the European Union, Luxembourg. [7]

INE (2020), *Resident population projections 2018-2080*, 31 March 2020, https://www.ine.pt/xportal/xmain?xpid=INE&xpgid=ine_destaques&DESTAQUESdest_boui=406534255&DESTAQUESmodo=2. [4]

INE (2014), *Resident population projections 2012-2060*, 28 March 2014, [6]
http://www.ine.pt/ngt_server/attachfileu.jsp?look_parentBoui=215593961&att_display=n&att_download=y (accessed on May 2021).

Jacobs-Crisioni, C., C. Perpiña Castillo, J.-P. Aurambout, C. Lavalle, C. Baranzelli, and F. [8]
Batista e Silva ((nd)), *Development of the LUISA Reference Scenario 2020 and Production of Fine-Resolution Population Projections by 5 Year Age Group*.

OECD (2021), *Delivering Quality Education and Health Care to All: Preparing Regions for* [9]
Demographic Change, OECD Rural Studies, OECD Publishing, Paris,
https://dx.doi.org/10.1787/83025c02-en.

OECD (2021), *OECD Regional Statistics*, https://www.oecd.org/regional/regional-statistics/ [1]
(accessed on May 2021).

OECD (2020), *Decentralisation and Regionalisation in Portugal*, OECD, [5]
https://doi.org/10.1787/fea62108-en (accessed on May 2021).

Statistics Portugal (2021), "Censos 2021", *Preliminary results*, [2]
https://censos.ine.pt/xportal/xmain?xpgid=censos21_main&xpid=CENSOS21&xlang=pt
(accessed on 22 September 2021).

Note

[1] Data from self-administered speed tests by Ookla is presented as deviations from the national average to highlight within-country differences in the quality of broadband connections.

3 Multi-level governance and subnational finance for service provision

Introduction

In Alentejo, a region with both the largest territory and the lowest population density in Portugal, population decline and ageing pose large challenges for local public service provision, in particular given the ongoing decentralisation reform in Portugal (OECD, 2020[1]). These demographic developments imply, lower demand for education services and higher demand for health care services, which, in turn, requires changes to local public service provision in the region and better articulation and coordination among levels of government. Ageing and population shrinking also puts strong pressure on municipal governments and parishes, confronted with ensuring access to quality public services while striving to maintain human resource and financial capacities.

To ensure an efficient provision of services in the face of demographic changes, municipalities, inter-municipal communities (IMCs) and parishes have a very important role to play. Joint actions and cooperation may facilitate mutual understanding among different entities and enable them to find solutions to the common challenges they face. The Regional Strategy for Alentejo 2030 (*Estratégia Regional Alentejo 2030*) take over this challenge, by including, for example, digital and shared solutions across municipalities through inter-municipal authorities (CCDR Alentejo, 2020[2]).

The multi-level governance system in Portugal has been undergoing important structural changes in recent years, and the success of these reforms will depend, to a large extent, on how municipalities can maintain quality public service delivery in the face of a shrinking population and labour force, and the erosion of tax bases. While the creation of inter-municipal communities and the gradual transfer of competences to municipalities support horizontal coordination, municipalities and parishes in Alentejo still face some limitations in effectively collaborating and ensuring efficient service delivery. The current multi-level governance framework and the financing of local authorities in Alentejo need some fine-tuning in order to make sure services are provided efficiently and at the right scale, given the region's sparsely populated areas.

This chapter examines the multi-level governance system in Alentejo, with a particular focus on inter-municipal co-operation for services provision, and the challenges brought by the ongoing decentralisation process. The second part of the chapter focuses on how municipalities, parishes and inter-municipal entities finance service provision and the main challenges they currently faced on this respect. Finally, the last section presents three policy recommendations for Alentejo's consideration, summarised in the following box.

Recommendations on multi-level governance and subnational finance for service provision

This box summarises the main recommendations on multi-level governance and subnational finance detailed in the Recommendations section.

Further pursuing decentralisation and regionalisation reforms to better align service provision and local needs

- At the local level: Accompany the transfer of competences to municipalities with the transfer of adequate financial resources. Incentives could be given to municipalities to take over more responsibilities, including receiving more fiscal resources (from grants) and powers (more own-source revenues).

- At the regional level: Pilot a new governance model in Alentejo, to organise it in a way that coincides with TL2 level, testing, for example, the model of cooperative regions as an alternative to, or an intermediate stage towards full regionalisation.

Strengthening cross-jurisdiction cooperation is necessary to make sure the planning and delivery of services are done at the right scale

- Provide concrete financial incentives to promote inter-municipal collaboration, for example, by directing more transfers to IMCs, instead of municipalities, particularly with respect to public services with important externalities

- Encourage peer-learning building on already successful inter-municipal co-operation mechanisms in the region

- Foster technical capacity through cooperation among parishes to enable them to effectively perform their tasks and deliver local services to residents and encourage parishes co-operation from different municipalities, if appropriate.

- Explore instances of co-operation with neighbouring regions and share knowledge with regions that face similar problems.

- Identify municipalities or groups of municipalities pertaining to the same functional area that could benefit the most from scaling-up the provision of services.

Adjusting fiscal arrangements to ensure municipalities can properly finance service provision and adapt to demographic trends

- Strengthen the municipal own revenue base in a gradual manner to enable municipalities to attract people and investments.

- Guarantee financial means of IMCs to particularly benefit small municipalities that have less capacity to raise own revenues.

The multi-level governance system for service provision in Alentejo

The multi-level governance system in Portugal

Based on the 1976 Constitution, Portugal has a three-tier system of subnational governments, consisting of regions, municipalities and parishes (Figure 3.1). At the local level there are 308 municipalities (*municípios*) – all of which have the same legal status - and 3 091 parishes (*freguesias*). In region of

DELIVERING QUALITY SERVICES TO ALL IN ALENTEJO © OECD 2022

Alentejo (TL2) there are five inter-municipal communities (*Comunidade inter-municipal,* IMCs) (Alentejo - Alentejo Central, Alentejo Litoral, Alto Alentejo, Baixo Alentejo, Lezíria do Tejo) and 58 municipalities; however, when considering Alentejo's administrative region, it is divided in four sub-regions (Alto Alentejo, Baixo Alentejo, Alentejo Central and Alentejo Litoral) and 47 municipalities. In fact, for statistical purposes Lezíria do Tejo is part of Alentejo, but for administrative purposes it is part of the administrative region of Lisboa e Vele do Tejo.

Portuguese municipalities are large in terms of population compared to other EU countries, with 90% of the population living in municipalities with more than 5 000 inhabitants and 40% with more than 20 000 inhabitants. In addition to the local administrative entities, the local public sector also comprises municipal and inter-municipal enterprises (MIEs), which are legally defined as business-like organisation. Their activities are restricted to general interest services, the management of collective equipment, the provision of services in the areas of education and companies of local and regional development.

Figure 3.1. Multi-level governance system in Portugal

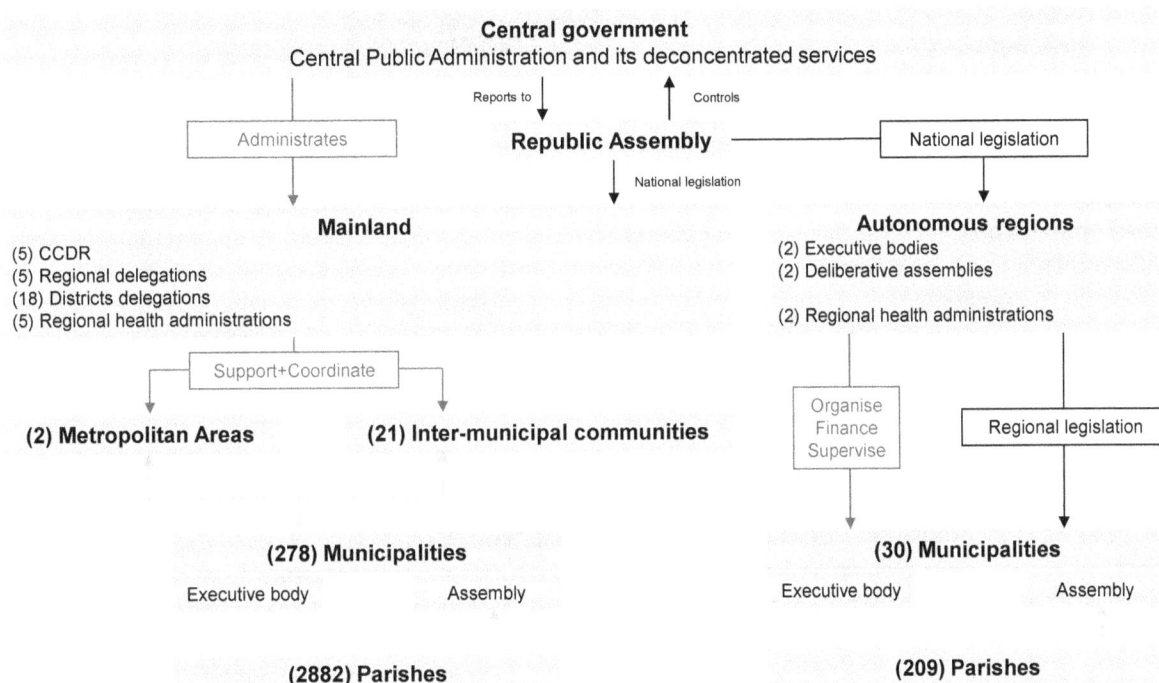

Note: Municipal and inter-municipal enterprises, as well as other organisational forms aimed at inter-institutional co-operation, are not included.
Source: (OECD, 2020[1])

At the regional level, while regionalisation is enshrined in the 1976 Constitution, mainland Portugal still does not have decentralised regions in place; only the islands of Acores and Madeira constitute autonomous regions in the country. In mainland Portugal, the process of regionalisation, based on the creation of eight elected regional governments (called "administrative regions"), was rejected in a 1998 referendum. Since then, regionalisation has continuously been debated and different models of regional governance have been discussed; however, they have not led to a concrete regional reform.

To manage policies at the regional level and co-ordinate the central government services at the regional scale, Portugal has established deconcentrated regional services, namely the Regional Coordination and Development Committees (*Comissão de Coordenação e Desenvolvimento Regional,* CCDR) (Box 3.1), regional delegations, districts delegations, and Regional Health Administrations. As explained above, in

Alentejo, the CCDR only covers four sub-regions – Lezíria do Tejo that for statistical purposes pertain to the TL2 regional definition, for administrative purposes it is part of the Lisbon region.

Box 3.1. Alentejo Regional Coordination and Development Commission (CCDR-A)

The Alentejo Regional Coordination and Development Commission (CCDR-A) is a deconcentrated service of central government integrated in the Ministry of the Territorial Cohesion and jointly managed by the Ministry of Environment and Climate Action (with regard to matters of environment and land use planning) and the Ministry for the Modernisation of the State and Public Administration (with regard to the relationship with local authorities). Its mission is to promote in an integrated and sustainable way the development of the Alentejo region.

According to Decree-Law no. 27/2020, of June 17, the CCDRs are headed by a president assisted by two vice presidents, all appointed by resolution of the Council of Ministers. The president is elected by an electoral college made up of several local elected representatives from the geographic area of action of the respective CCDR. A vice-president is appointed by the presidents of the municipal councils that comprise the geographic area covered by the respective CCDR; another vice-president is appointed by the Government, on the proposal of the member of the Government responsible for territorial cohesion, in prior coordination with the members of the Government responsible for the areas of local authorities and the environment, after consulting the already appointed president and vice-president

The CCDR-A has administrative and financial autonomy and is tasked with coordinating and promoting governmental policies regarding regional planning and development, environment, land management, inter-regional and cross-border cooperation. For this, the Commission is a Managing Authority for the Regional Operational Programme funded by the European Union, as well as other regional development financing instruments. The CCDR-A is also in charge of providing technical support to local authorities and their associations.

Source: (CCDR-A, 2021[3])

The role of the Regional Coordination and Development Committee of Alentejo (*Comissão de Coordenação e Desenvolvimento Regional do Alentejo,* CCDR Alentejo) is crucial. Municipalities do not have the critical mass to operate at the regional level and municipal mergers are not desirable given that municipalities are already large and not densely populated, particularly in Alentejo. IMCs are an adequate level to provide joint services but do not cover the appropriate scale for regional development policies. The CCDR that facilitates a mutual understanding among municipalities and IMCs in order to find a regional-level framework and better take into account challenges identified by IMCs in their strategies, for example regarding the sharing of equipment.

Between the regional and municipal levels, the metropolitan areas (*área metropolitana*) of Lisbon and Porto and the 21 inter-municipal communities (*Comunidade inter-municipal,* IMCs*),* created by Law 75/2013, constitute the basis of the NUTS3 statistical regions. The IMCs and Metropolitan Areas are constituted by contract and any municipality that is part of a territorial unit where an IMC already exists has the right to adhere to it. Currently, all municipalities are engaged in one of the inter-municipal cooperative associations in Portugal and there are five in Alentejo – Alentejo Central, Alentejo Litoral, Alto Alentejo, Baixo Alentejo, and Lezíria do Tejo. IMCs are governed by the inter-municipal assembly (deliberative power), the inter-municipal council, the Executive Secretariat (executive power), and the Strategic council for inter-municipal development (advisory power). IMCs can only provide services that are assigned to them by municipalities and the central government (OECD, 2020[1]).

While the CCDR helps in bringing clarity and enabling co-ordination at the regional level, it is still challenging to coordinate sectoral, territorial and regional policies in Alentejo. The multiplicity of sectoral actors at different levels of government make this articulation and co-ordination challenging, having a direct impact in the ability to implement place-based policies. For instance, health services are organised by the central administration around the NUTS2 level (and central healthcare centres) while other services such as home affairs, or social security are organised at the local level. In the case of education, responsibilities are shared between the central and local levels, in particular for the definition of the curricula. While the local level manages up to 25% of the curricula, the Ministry of Education at the central level sets the remaining percentage of the curricula and supervises schools.

The central level plays an important role in service provision

Despite the ongoing decentralisation reform, the Portuguese central government still plays a strong role in public service provision and has significant responsibilities in education, health, and social services. The spending structure of Portuguese subnational governments contrast with OECD and EU countries. In Portugal, the main subnational sectoral spending categories as a percentage of GDP are general services (1.6%) and economic affairs (0.9%), whereas in the European Union (EU) the main sector spending categories are social protection and education (Figure 3.2). Local government spending as a percentage of GDP in education (0.7%) and health (0.4%) are significantly below EU averages (1.8% and 1.5% respectively).

While municipal responsibilities have been relatively stable over the last 20 years, in 2015, Law 69/2015 expanded their competencies in education, teaching and vocational training. The role of municipalities in education has been growing over the past years. In pre-primary and basic schools, for example, municipalities are responsible for providing extracurricular activities, school meals and transport, and for compensating non-teaching staff (OECD, 2020[1]). Since 2017, Portugal is implementing a curricula reform process, introducing higher levels of autonomy and flexibility at the local level in order to improve school ability to design and carry out curricula solutions adapted to its own context. Since 2018, the central level is not the only responsible for setting up the curricula and all schools are able to manage up to 25% of it. Moreover, the decentralisation programme approved in 2019 – which will cover all municipalities in 2022, transfers the schools budget to municipalities. This means that former national administration expenses with schools will be transferred to municipalities to be managed locally. Municipalities may also allocate additional funds according to local projects and programmes. The central level is still responsible for setting a part of the curricula, teacher recruitment and setting wages.

Figure 3.2. Local government expenditure by function (COFOG), 2019

As a percentage of GDP

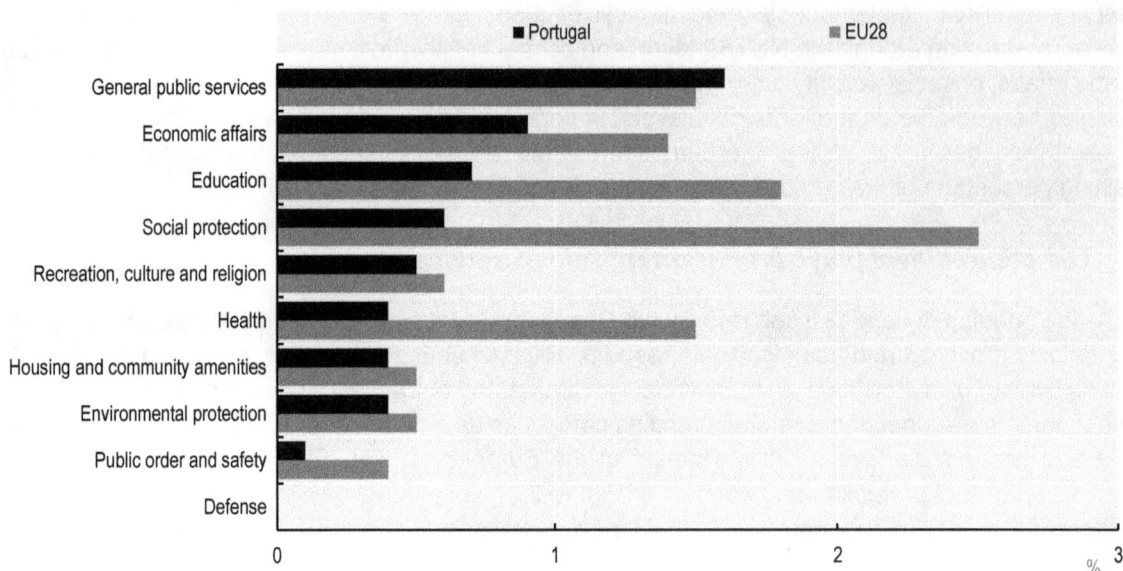

Source: (Eurostat, 2021[4]), *General government expenditure by function (COFOG),* https://ec.europa.eu/eurostat/databrowser/view/GOV_10A_EXP/default/table?lang=en (accessed on 30 October 2021).

While the parishes' competences are somewhat limited, they still play a role in service provision as they can act as delegated units of the municipality for service delivery. The decree-law 57/2019, allows, if both parts agree, the possibility of a redistribution of competences and financial resources from the municipality to the parish. These transfers can be agreed for the management and maintenance of green spaces, cleaning of public spaces and maintenance of urban furniture, fairs and markets, and maintenance of school spaces. Still, the delegation of competences from the municipal to the parish level is challenging as parishes do not necessarily have the appropriate means – in terms of human and financial resources - to take over those responsibilities. At the same time, municipalities are struggling with decentralising themselves as more competences are being transferred to them without the necessary additional financial support – while the transfers are significant, they do not necessarily cover all the increasing management costs associated with the transfer of competences (see below). In Alentejo, some municipalities, particularly in the North, declare that they face difficulties in decentralising competencies to parishes in a homogeneous way.

The increasing role of inter-municipal entities in public service provision

The Portuguese law foresees different figures to allow and encourage inter-municipal and inter-parishes associations. Inter-municipal entities (metropolitan areas and inter-municipal communities) enable municipal cooperation in various strategic areas where local service delivery may benefit from increasing scale and improved inter-governmental coordination. The transfer of competences to municipalities in a low-density territory confronted with shrinking and ageing population such as Alentejo needs to come hand in hand with the up-scaling of certain services. This holds true when it comes to minimise the shortcomings related to low and unequal levels of administrative (human and financial) capacities of local administrations.

Municipalities can delegate tasks to IMCs and parishes and can make contractual arrangements with the central government to exercise shared responsibilities (OECD-UCLG, 2019[5]). IMCs have tasks in regional planning and development, in the provision of essential public services, and in ensuring articulation between municipalities and central administration services in various domains, such as educational and vocational training networks, public equipment network, mobility and transport (Box 3.2)

Box 3.2. Inter-municipal communities in Portugal

Inter-municipal communities (IMCs), which are organised at the NUTS 3 level, can assume functions and tasks assigned by law to the municipalities. However, IMCs can only provide services that are assigned to them by municipalities and the central government. In the current legal framework, IMCs are designed to pursue the following assignments:

1. Promoting the planning and management of the strategy for economic, social and environmental protection of its territory.
2. Co-ordinating municipal investments of inter-municipal interest.
3. Participating in the management of regional development programmes.
4. Planning the activities of public entities, with a supra-municipal character.

It is also the responsibility of the IMC to ensure the co-ordination of actions between municipalities and central government in the following areas:

1. Public supply networks, basic sanitation infrastructures, treatment of wastewater and municipal waste
2. Network of health equipment
3. Educational and vocational training network
4. Spatial planning, nature conservation and natural resources
5. Security and civil protection
6. Mobility and transport
7. Public equipment networks
8. Promotion of economic, social and cultural development
9. Network of cultural, sports and leisure equipment

Source: (OECD, 2020[1])

In Portugal, the EU Cohesion Policy has reinforced the financial and strategic capacities of IMCs. They currently manage European Cohesion Policy funding as intermediate bodies and their strategic role for service provision is one of the key objectives of the current programing period. In addition, as intermediate bodies, they are also key for territorial investment; the programming of integrated territorial investments by IMCs and metropolitan areas through the Pacts for Development and Territorial Cohesion (PDCT) within the framework of Portugal 2020 (Forum das Cidades, 2020[6]). In this framework, some IMCs conduct projects that are key to promote regional development. The IMC of Alentejo Litoral for example, is carrying out an inter-municipal climate change adaptation plan and five urban resilience plans, one for each Municipality of Alentejo Litoral. They are also in the process of mapping social, health and educational services within its territory. IMCs have also served to ensure that municipalities co-operate to develop the specific strategies within their territory responding to specific territorial needs. This is the case, for example, of co-ordination of vocational programmes, for which the national level aims at ensuring this co-ordination happens. This is what happens in the project involving Almodovar, Mértola, Castro Verde, Aljustrel and Ourique municipality that have developed a vocational training offer to match the labour market needs and to articulate the students' mobility services, as a mean of preventing both desertification and students' dropout.

Municipalities can also pursue their tasks through other organisational forms aimed at inter-institutional cooperation and involve public, private and social partners (OECD, 2020[1]), namely cooperatives and foundations, or associations. For example, Lezíria do Tejo has established two inter-municipal companies a water utility company and a waste treatment company. This allowed rationalising public services provision in these areas. The water utility company is profitable and municipalities have decided to promote further investments instead of collecting the dividends. The associations of parishes and municipalities with specific purposes are created to promote certain projects of common interest to their members, such as the *Associação de municípios do Alentejo Central* or the *Associação de municípios para a gestão da água pública no Alentejo* which aims at guaranteeing the quality, continuity and efficiency of public services of water collection treatment and supply for public consumption and the collection, treatment and disposal of urban waste water (ANMP, 2021[7]).

Alentejo also benefits from cross-border co-operation enhanced by the EU. The cooperation programme Interreg V-A Spain Portugal (POCTEP) aims at tackling cross-border challenges and promoting smart and sustainable growth. It also seeks to foster territorial cohesion by developing and improving cross-border public services along the Spanish – Portuguese border. Alentejo, Algarve, Centro and Norte NUTS2 regions (Portugal) and Andalucía, Castilla y León, Extremadura and Galicia Autonomous Communities (Spain) participate in this project financed by Regional Development Fund (ERDF, EUR 365 million).

The current multi-level governance framework does not allow to deliver services with region-wide benefits, such healthcare or transport – the latter being provided at the IMC level. Moreover, while IMCs have proven to be essential for the functioning of the multi-level governance system, in some cases it has been difficult to stimulate participation of municipalities in IMCs projects as they do not necessarily see the advantages of supra-municipal coordination. In addition, since decision making by inter-municipal communities requires unanimity among municipalities, the line of actions and investment by IMCs remains limited.

Although today Portugal does not envisage providing municipalities or municipal associations new taxing powers, the French experience is an example of innovative ways of promoting IMCs. The French government has persistently supported inter-municipal co-operation by giving some Public Establishments for Inter-municipal Cooperation (EPCI, *Établissement Public de Coopération Intercommunale*) -a form of IMC created in 1992- their own sources of revenues and taxing powers to exercise some of their mandatory municipal competences or some other voluntary tasks agreed by all the municipalities involved (OECD, 2017[8]). Reflecting on this experience, Alentejo could find ways to give IMCs more powers or flexibility to carry out their functions. Indeed, while the local autonomy on taxation is bounded by the Portuguese Constitution, there is an ongoing process of sharing taxes between different administration levels and a growing level of flexibility for municipalities to use a % of key national taxes, as IRS, IMI, IVA. Providing with more flexibility to the IMCs on this regard could also be envisaged.

Opportunities and challenges of the ongoing decentralisation process

Since 2018, Portugal has embarked in an important decentralisation process (Law No. 50/2018) which stipulates the transfer of responsibilities to local authorities and inter-municipal entities between 2019 and 2022. Municipalities have gradually adhered to this Law since 2019 and those that have not adhered yet will have to do so by 2022. In the field of education, all competences that refer to non-tertiary education, except the management of teaching staff and the definition of curricular contents, is being transferred to municipalities.

Box 3.3. The ongoing decentralisation reform in Portugal

In order to clarify the assignments and responsibilities, and to take steps for further decentralisation, Law no. 50/2018 of 16 August defined the framework for the transfers of new additional competencies to local authorities. The transfer of competencies started in 2019 for the local authorities that did not declare, until 15 September, that they were not willing to implement them.

The decentralisation Law has two main axes:

1. The reorganisation of the state at the regional and sub-regional levels, only in the continental part of the country.
2. The transfer of new competencies from the government to the municipalities, a transfer that in some cases can be for the IMC, aiming to strengthen inter-municipal structures.

Regarding the first dimension, the political decision has no fixed schedule. Regarding the competencies to be transferred to the municipalities, Law no. 50/2018 defined a wide range of new competencies to be transferred until January 2021. For education, health and social action, the deadline has been extended to March 2022. The specific conditions of these transfers, namely financial conditions, are currently being clarified. In general terms, the areas transferred to municipalities are:

1. Education, all that refers to non-tertiary education, except management of teaching staff and definition of curricular contents.
2. Social action at the local level, especially in the fight against poverty.
3. Justice: "Julgados de Paz" network (volunteer commitment court), social reintegration and support for victims of crimes.
4. Health, local equipment and management of non-clinical personnel.
5. Municipal civil protection.
6. Culture, local heritage and museums not classified as national.
7. State unused real estate assets.
8. Housing, housing of the state and management of urban rental and rehabilitation programmes.
9. Management of port-maritime areas: secondary fishing ports, recreational boating and urban areas for tourism development.
10. Tourism (inter-municipal entities): management of investment funds, planning and subregional tourism promotion.
11. Investment attraction and management of community funds (intermunicipal entities): definition of the territorial strategy for development and management of local development programmes with community funding.
12. Beaches: licensing, management and equipment of sea, river and lake beaches integrated in the public domain of the state.
13. Management of forests and protected areas.
14. Transport: infrastructures and equipment within urban perimeters.
15. Citizen service: citizen's shops.
16. Proximity policing, participation in the definition of a policing model.
17. Protection and animal health.
18. Food safety.
19. Fire safety in buildings.

20. Public parking: regulation, supervision and management of administrative misconduct.

21. Licensing games of chance and fortune at a local level.

Source: (OECD, 2020[1])

The transfer of competences from the central level to municipalities has represented an opportunity for local governments, who have been able to reorganise, to a certain extent, the provision of public services. In Alentejo, for example, decentralising tasks associated with transport services permitted to facilitate the reorganisation of the network, and in some cases, to close small schools and reorganise the delivery of school transportation and education services in a more rational way with one school providing education services for different places.

However, the transfer of competences has also been somewhat burdensome for local governments. As is the case in many OECD countries, the transfers of funds do not necessarily follows the transfers of competences and funding remains below what is needed by municipalities to efficiently deliver on their new tasks. Certainly, by Law, the funds directly associated with the tasks being transferred need to be reallocated to the local level. However, these funds do not consider the additional administrative costs that municipalities need to incur when dealing with new tasks, including adjustments in functions in order to deliver new tasks and new, often onerous, administrative procedures, for example, requiring adjusting municipal contracts with electricity providers.

In addition, the incomplete decentralisation process, and in particular the lack of a regional level, also affects the efficient provision of services in Alentejo. The lack of a regional level of government may hinder the provision of certain services as the central government might be too large and municipalities too small to deliver services effectively. This situation contrasts, for example, with the neighbouring regions in Spain, where the regional-level has a significant amount of autonomous decision making capacity in education and health care service provision and investment.

Financing local public services in Alentejo

While the fiscal framework of local authorities has undergone reforms in recent years (2007, 2013, 2018) to strengthen municipal finance and improve its sustainability, the fiscal situation of Portuguese municipalities, in particular in Alentejo, is challenging   First, the transition from a centrally financed model to a model which is based on greater self-reliance at the subnational government level has been slow. In addition, while direct and shared tax revenues represent a significant share of municipal revenues, municipal tax bases in Alentejo tend to be below the national average. In addition, central government transfers to municipalities, in particular capital transfers, have decreased after 2010 (OECD, 2020[1]), resulting from national fiscal consolidation measures. Finally, ageing and shrinking population put at stake the current funding models of local public services in Portugal.

To address challenges facing local public service delivery in Alentejo, the funding model of sub-regional and local authorities should give more room for local initiatives and fiscal incentives fostering the attractiveness of rural areas.

Portugal is one of the most centralised countries of the OECD

Portugal is one of the most centralised countries in the OECD. The strong role of the central government in public service provision is reflected in the responsibilities devolved to subnational governments. In 2019, subnational governments expenditure accounted for 13,5% of total public spending, compared with 40,2% on average in OECD countries, and 33,6% on average in the EU (see Figure 3.3). In education, health services and social services, the central government bears the main responsibility in Portugal (OECD, 2020[1]). As was pointed before, compared with the EU average, the spending assignments of Portuguese subnational governments differ markedly. While in the EU, the three largest sectoral spending categories are social protection, education and general services, in Portugal the main local services comprise general services, economic affairs and other services (see Figure 3.2).

Figure 3.3. Subnational government expenditure as a percentage of GDP and total public expenditure, 2019

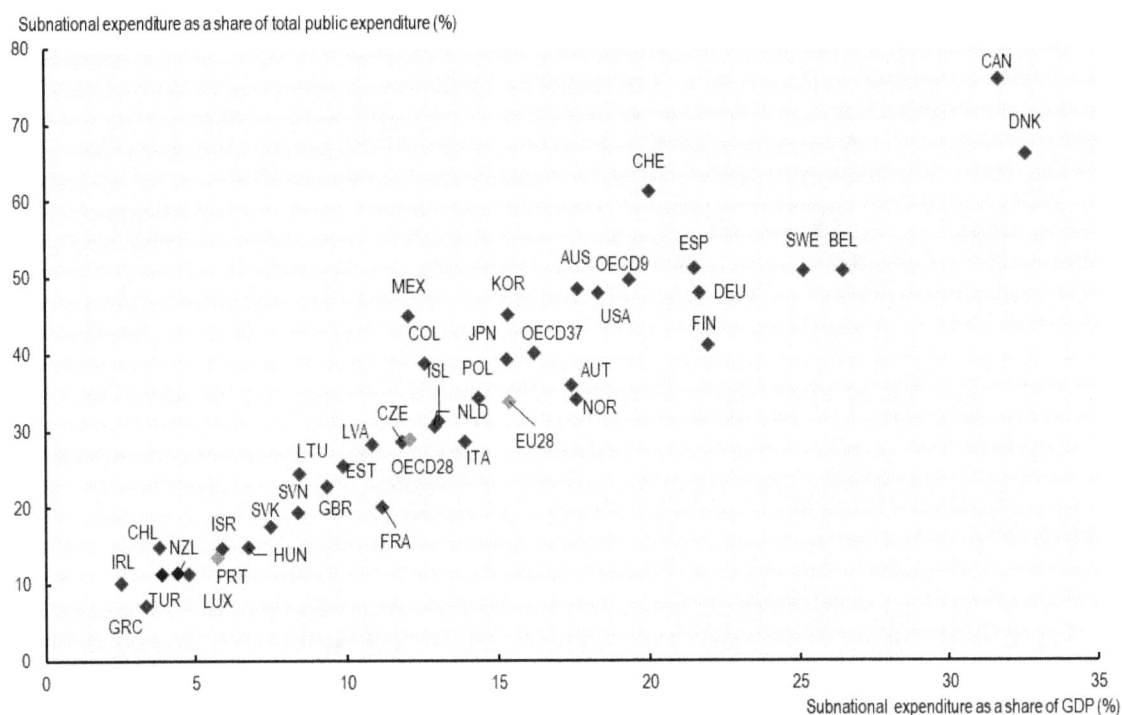

Note: Australia, Chile and Colombia: estimates from IMF Government Finance Statistics. 2018 data for Chile, Japan, New Zealand, Turkey
Source: (OECD, 2021[9])

Subnational government revenue is also below the OECD average. In 2019, Portuguese subnational government revenue represented 14.1% of total public revenue and 6% of GDP, below the OECD average (42.2% and 15.7% respectively) and the EU average (34.2% and 15.4% respectively).

Figure 3.4. Subnational government revenue as a percentage of GDP and total public revenue, 2019

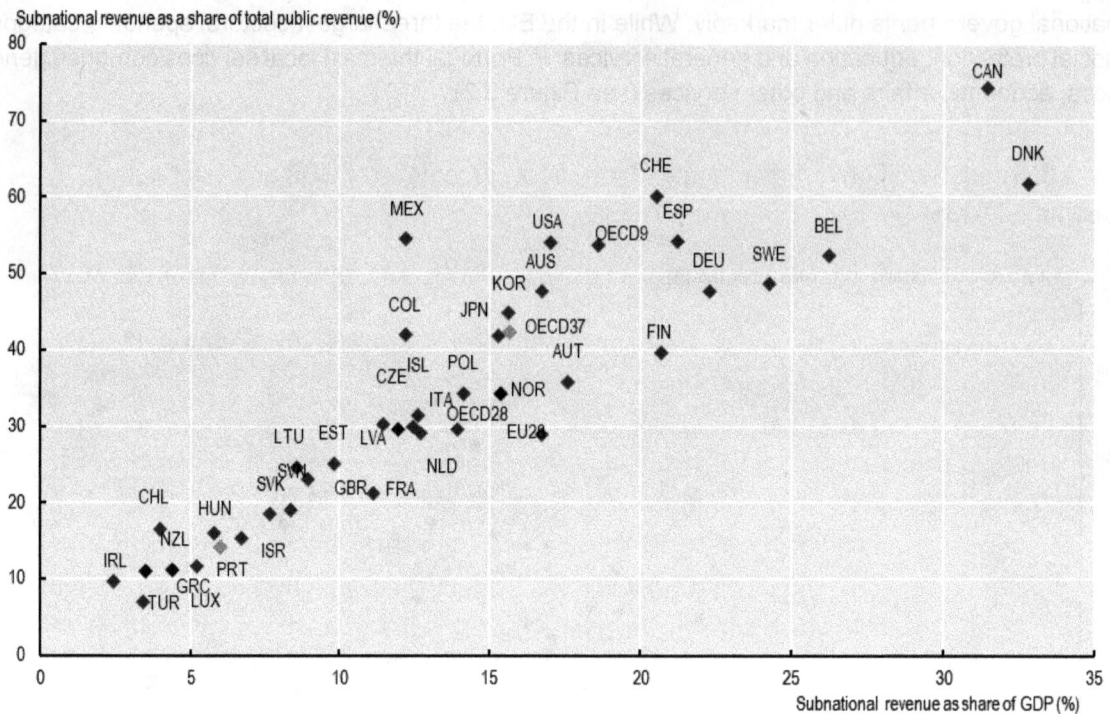

Note: Australia, Chile and Colombia: estimates from IMF Government Finance Statistics. 2018 data for Chile, Japan, New Zealand, Turkey
Source: (OECD, 2021[9])

Although the share of tax revenues in subnational revenue is at the same level of the EU average (41% in 2019) and the share of grants lower than the EU average (34% vs 45%) thanks to a high share of revenues from user charges and tariffs, they have little fiscal autonomy. In Alentejo, municipalities have even weaker fiscal space. They rely significantly on central government transfers and their tax revenues is not necessarily optimised.

Figure 3.5. Structure of subnational revenue, 2019 (%)

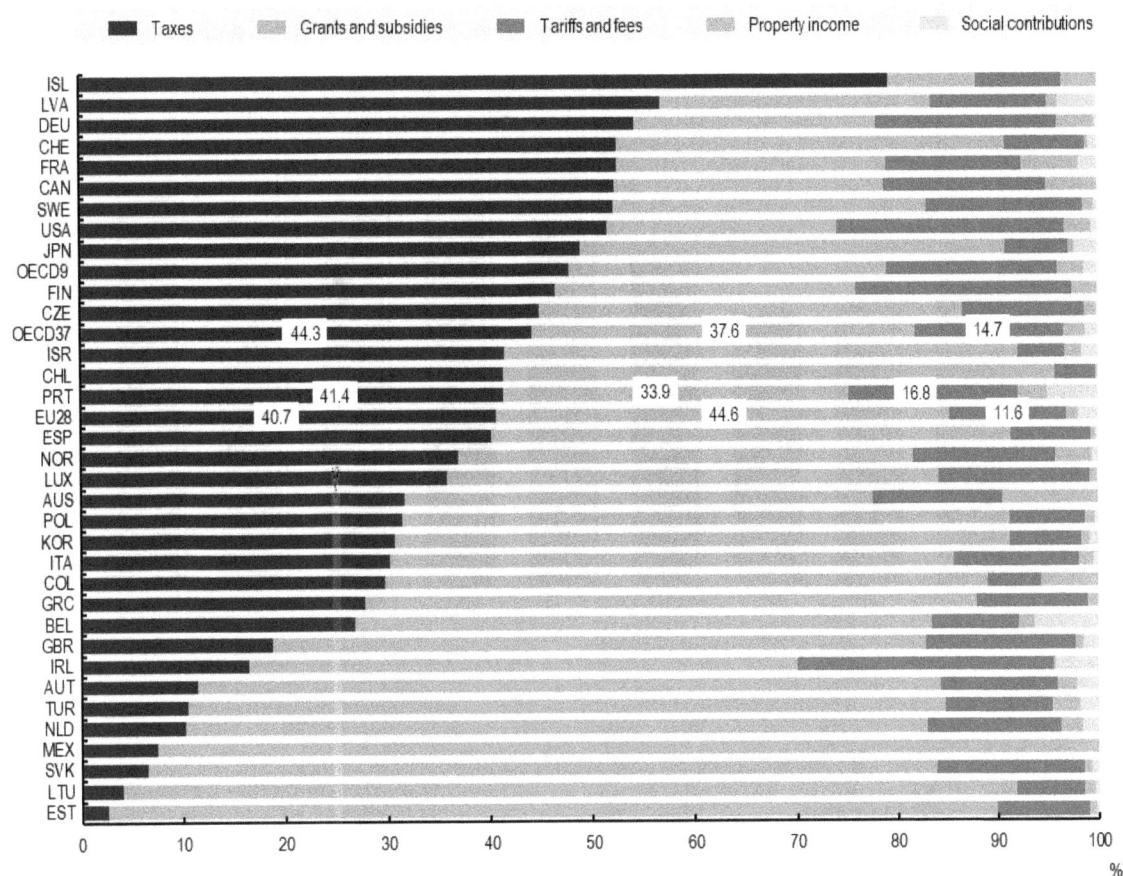

Note: Australia, Chile and Colombia: estimates from IMF Government Finance Statistics. 2018 data for Chile, Japan, New Zealand, Turkey
Source: (OECD, 2021[9])

Municipalities in Alentejo strongly rely on central government transfers

In Alentejo, intergovernmental transfers are the main source of revenues for municipalities. In 2019, on average, current transfers represented 47.3% of total revenues for municipalities and capital transfers were about 12.8% of total revenues. Among these transfers, 88.2% corresponded to transfers from the central government, 9.8% were Community Funds (EU transfers) and the remaining 2% to other transfers from other public entities and private transfers. Interestingly, since 2010, the composition of municipal revenues has changed. The share of current transfers increased from 37.8% to 47.3% between 2010 and 2019, while the share of capital transfers decreased from 26.5% to 12.7%. The decline in capital transfers is mainly the result of lower capital transfers from the Financial Equilibrium Fund (FEF) and Participation in Community co-financed projects, with implications on municipalities' investment capacity.

Figure 3.6. Composition of municipal revenue from current transfers, Alentejo

By counterpart, in Euros, 2010-2019

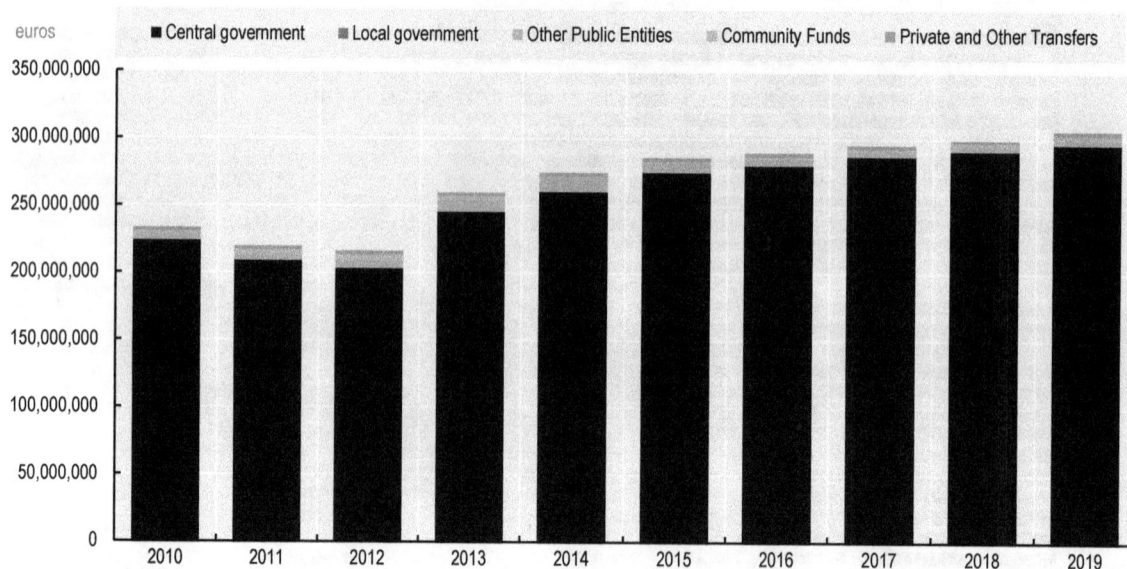

Source: (DGAL, 2021[10]), *Regime financeiro das autarquias locais*, http://www.portalautarquico.dgal.gov.pt/pt-PT/financas-locais/ (accessed on 30 October 2021).

Figure 3.7. Composition of municipal revenue from capital transfers, Alentejo

By counterpart, in Euros, 2010-2019

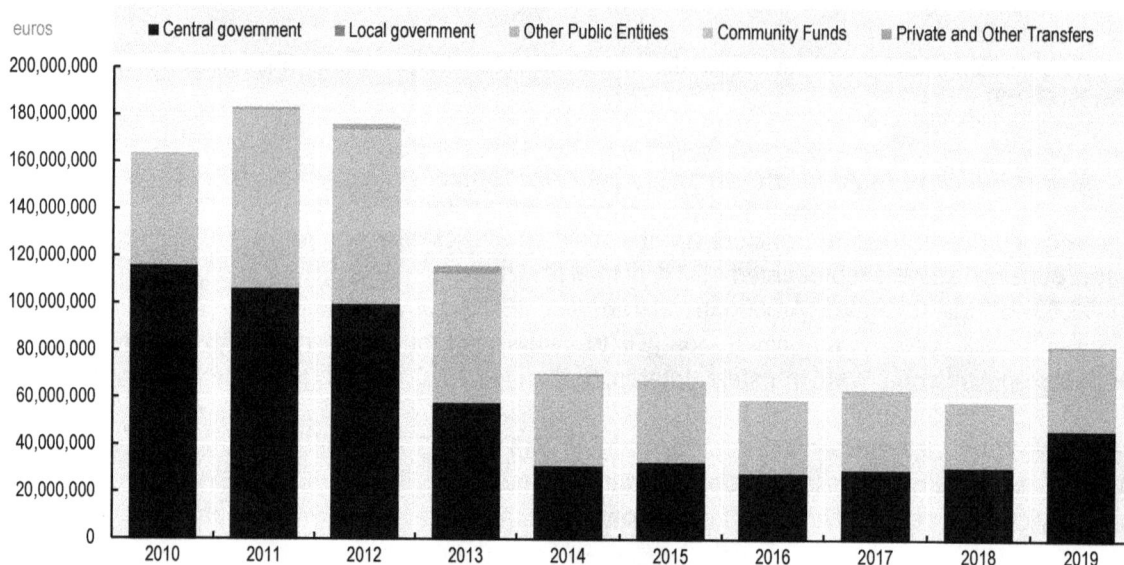

Note: Central government capital transfers mostly consist of the Financial Equilibrium Fund.
Source: (DGAL, 2021[10]), *Regime financeiro das autarquias locais*, http://www.portalautarquico.dgal.gov.pt/pt-PT/financas-locais/ (accessed on 30 October 2021).

Figure 3.8. Composition of municipal revenue from capital transfers, Alentejo

By type, in Euros, 2010-2019

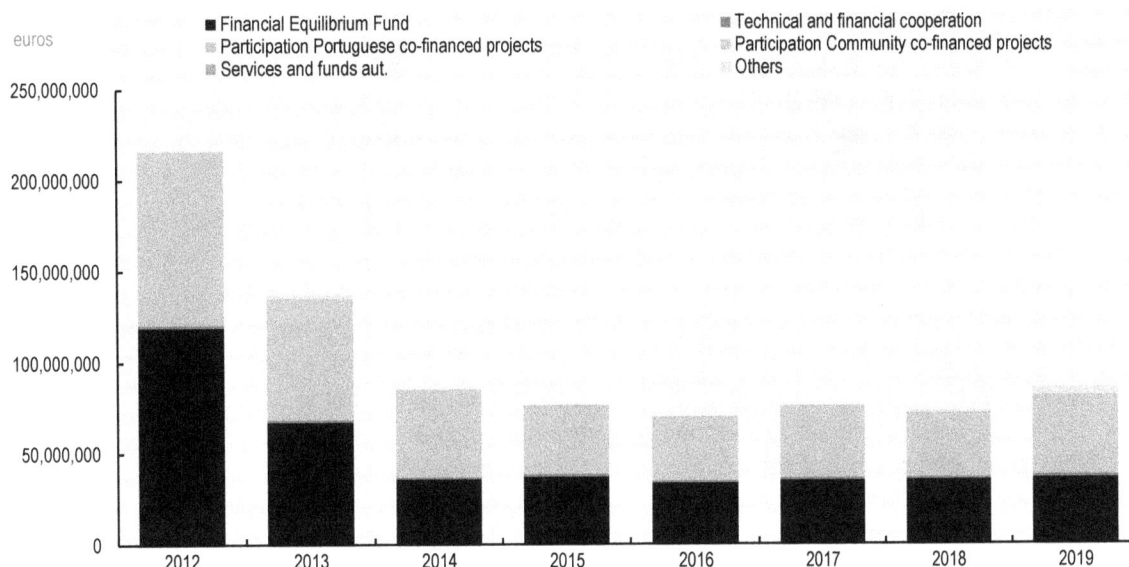

Source: (DGAL, 2021[10]), *Regime financeiro das autarquias locais*, http://www.portalautarquico.dgal.gov.pt/pt-PT/financas-locais/ (accessed on 30 October 2021).

Figure 3.9. Composition of municipal revenue, Alentejo

In Euros, 2010-2019

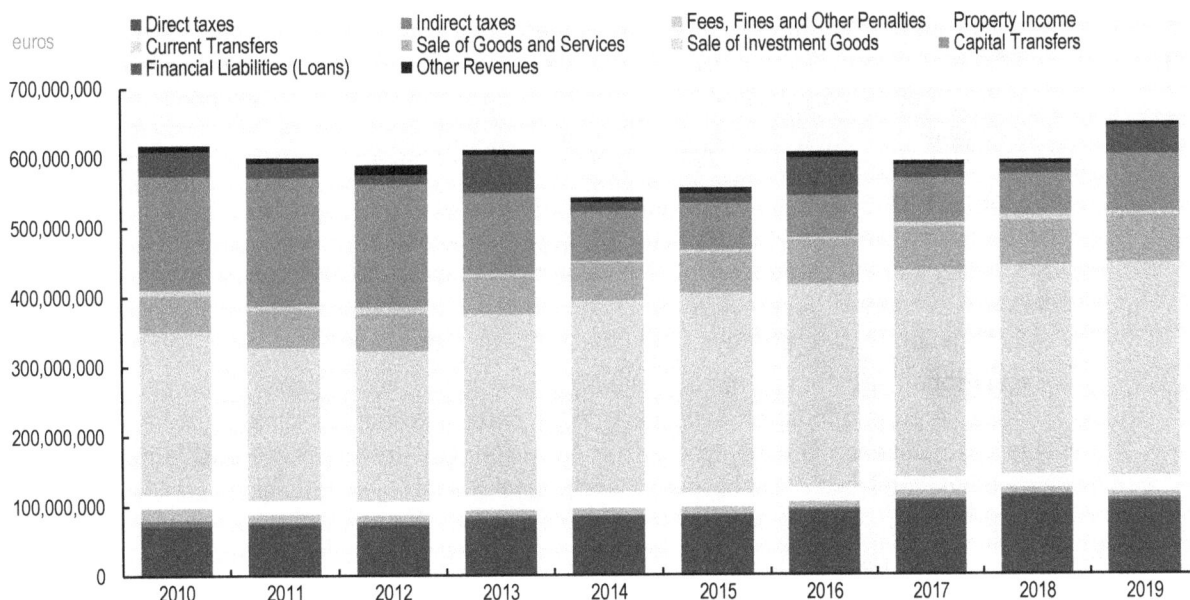

Source: (DGAL, 2021[10]), *Regime financeiro das autarquias locais*, http://www.portalautarquico.dgal.gov.pt/pt-PT/financas-locais/ (accessed on 30 October 2021).

The most important component of intergovernmental transfers are transfers resulting from tax sharing, which are particularly important for inland municipalities. On average, inland municipalities receive higher values of tax sharing transfers than those from the coastline. Since 2007, pursuing the objectives of horizontal and vertical financial balance, tax sharing transfers include:

- A general-purpose grant, the Financial Equilibrium Fund (FEF), whose value is equal to 19.5% of the simple arithmetic average of income from personal income tax (IRS), the corporate income tax and value added tax (VAT). This fund is then divided into two sub-funds with different purposes and subsequently redistributed among municipalities with different criteria:
  - o Municipal General Fund – to finance their legal assignments. It is distributed according to population, surface area, and other cost factors.
  - o Municipal Cohesion Fund – with the objective of correcting asymmetries among municipalities, particularly with respect to fiscal capacity and unbalance of opportunities. Its allocation is based on municipal tax capacity and an index of municipal social development.
- A specific subsidy (earmarked grant), the Municipal Social Fund (FSM), whose value corresponds to the expenses related to the attributions and competences transferred from the central administration to the municipalities. It is a conditional transfer from the national budget designed to adjust to the transfer of additional assignments related to social functions such as health, education, and social assistance.
- A 7.5% share of VAT revenue collected in the accommodation, catering, communications, electricity, water and gas sectors.
- A Decentralisation Financing Fund (*Fundo de Financiamento de Descentralização*) to finance the new powers of local authorities (Law no. 73/2013 and Law no. 51/2018).

Municipal tax revenue comes from both shared taxation and own-sources taxes

Fiscal revenues are the most important component of municipal own revenues, besides user charges and fees. The main taxes that municipalities collect are the following:

- Municipal Property Tax (*Imposto Municipal sobre Imóveis,* IMI), that was established in 2003 and replaced the Municipal Contribution. The IMI's rates are set annually by the municipalities in the area where properties are located within the following range: between 0.3% and 0.45% for urban buildings (up to 0.5% in specific circumstances), and 0.8% for rural properties. The importance of IMI has been increasing over time as a result of the real estate tax reform implemented to increase local government's revenues. The reform led to a reduction of the temporary exemptions applicable to own housing and to a revaluation of urban real estate assets for taxation purposes, approximating it to the market value. The value revaluation has only concerned urban properties that is, rural properties have not yet been revaluated. This has impacted the differences in the capacity to generate own revenues from urban and rural municipalities.
- Municipal Property Purchase Tax (*Imposto Municipal sobre Transmissões Onerosas de Imóveis -* IMT) that entered into force on January 1, 2004 to replace the Municipal Sisa Tax. The rate is variable, and depends on the type of property (primary residence versus rental or holiday residence) and the value of the property. Since 2014, the IMT has been rising steadily.
- Surcharge tax (*Derrama*), a municipal tax on corporate income that is taxable by the national corporate income tax. This tax decreased considerably during the 2009 financial crisis, but since 2016 it has been increasing.
- Circulation Unique Tax (*Imposto Único de Circulação* – IUC), which revenues are shared among the central government and local governments. The IUC is a yearly tax that is calculated considering the engine cubic capacity (displacement) and the CO_2 emissions.
- A variable participation of 5% in the IRS, determined under the terms of article 26, of taxable persons with tax domicile in the respective territorial area, calculated on the respective collection net of the deductions.

Municipalities scope for setting tax rates is restricted at best, but some municipalities, particularly those with lower fiscal capacity, tend to adopt lower tax rates in the Property Tax (IMI) and Surcharge Tax (OECD, 2020[1]), in the use of their freedom to explore legal fiscal limits. While this behaviour can be understood as a way to attract private investments and promote economic development, it also creates greater disparities on the fiscal capacity of municipalities within the region and Portugal, making those with lower fiscal capacity even more dependent on central transfers. In Alentejo, municipal direct tax revenue mainly comes from the Municipal Property Tax (IMI) and the Municipal Tax on Onerous Property Transfers (IMT) (Figure 3.10).

Table 3.1. Municipal direct taxes, charged by the central administration

Tax Name	Tax base	Scope for setting tax rates	Weight in municipal tax revenue (%)	Weight in total municipal revenue (%)
Municipal Property Tax (IMI)	The municipal property tax (IMI) is levied on the taxable patrimonial value of rural and urban properties located in Portuguese territory.	Restricted	51.44	8.57
Municipal Tax on Onerous Property Transfers (IMT)	The IMT is levied on the transfers, for consideration, of the property right or partial figures of this right, on immovable property located in the national territory.	No room for manoeuvre	29.05	4.97
Single Circulation Tax (IUC)	The single circulation tax is levied on vehicles registered or registered in Portugal	No room for manoeuvre	10.08	1.69
Surcharge tax	The Surcharge is translated into the application of a tax on taxable income subject to Corporate Income Tax.	Restricted	9.39	1.6
IRS - Personal Income Tax	Personal income	0%-5% variable Some leeway		

Figure 3.10. Detailed composition of municipal direct tax revenue, Alentejo

In Euros, 2015-2019

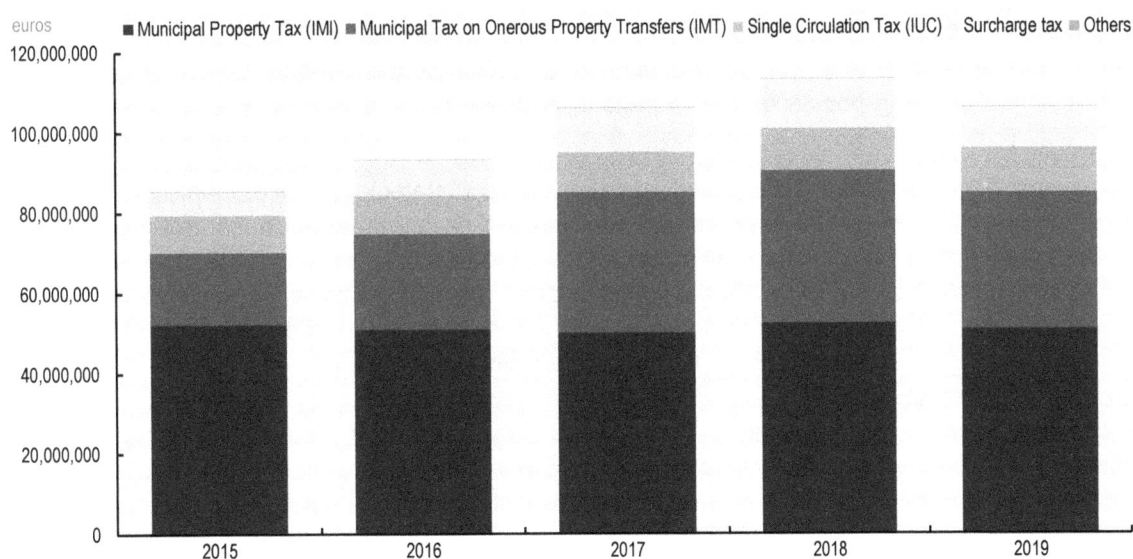

Source: (DGAL, 2021[10]), *Regime financeiro das autarquias locais*, http://www.portalautarquico.dgal.gov.pt/pt-PT/financas-locais/ (accessed on 30 October 2021).

The financing of parishes and inter-municipal entities is limited

The parishes and IMCs financing models limit their capacity to effectively provide services to the local community. On the one hand, parishes' own-revenues are based on a small fraction of property tax (IMI) and user charges related to some public services they provide. Parishes are also entitled to a general-purpose grant, the Financial Fund of Parishes, which corresponds to 2% of the average of the amount collected with personal income tax, corporate tax, and value-added tax (OECD, 2020[1]). Parishes have also limited access to EU funds; while leasing is allowed, they can only access short-term debt to face treasury difficulties (to be repaid at the year-end) and have no access to debt instruments for investment. However, as highlighted during the study mission, these source of financing remain limited and are at risk given the demographic changes of many municipalities in the region. This also means that parishes' investment depends on their ability to generate savings.

Similarly, IMCs across Portugal have only a restricted capacity to raise own revenues and are mainly financed by municipalities that are part of the community and transfers from the Financial Equilibrium Fund (FEF) which represent only 0.5% of the total FEF transfers. The limited financial means of these entities puts pressure on their capacity to be effective service providers. Diversifying funding sources of IMCS, as well as increasing the amount of transfer they perceive are crucial to enhance their functioning and expand their areas of intervention – which, in Alentejo, are mostly focused on transportation issues. This is also a way of encouraging municipalities to delegate tasks to IMCs.

An ageing and shrinking population jeopardises service delivery funding in Alentejo

As explained in detail in Chapter 2, Alentejo faces ageing and shrinking population, which impact directly (i) the type of services that local governments need to finance, as well as (ii) the local governments' capacity to finance the provision of services. The ongoing change of Alentejo's demographic structure will have a strong impact on education, health and long-term care services, but also on public infrastructure. Given the ageing trend, it is expected that public spending on age-related programs will increase. At the same time, the declining population is likely to have a negative effect on economic activity, resulting in a slowdown in public revenue growth. Shrinking population also means shrinking municipal tax bases. This represents an important challenge for services financing in Alentejo, where direct and shared taxes revenue account for a large share of total subnational government's revenue. Given the design of the transfer system, declining population also means a reduction of the transfers received from the central level.

Local governments across the OECD have adopted different strategies to face shrinking population. In Finland, for example, where rural and remote municipalities have suffered from shrinking population for many decades the state grant system has protected municipalities from a financial collapse. This has been despite the fact the grants are based on per capita calculations, and therefore the transfers decline as the population declines. However, the equalisation of the tax base and the spending needs calculations, which are largely based on the demographic structure of municipalities, have ensured that municipalities with shrinking population have not faced radical changes in revenue. Municipalities have also adjusted their spending and increased their income and property tax rates and used more debt funding. The central government has encouraged municipalities to improve efficiency in welfare services, especially by promoting voluntary municipal mergers and inter-municipal cooperation (OECD, forthcoming[11]). This is what has been partially done since 2013 in Portugal (Law 73/2013) which also protects municipalities of minimum growth and redistribution to municipalities with the lowest local tax rate).In Sweden, where the municipalities also have important service responsibilities, municipalities have responded to population decline by cutbacks in spending and increased efficiency, especially by school closures, as well as inter-municipal collaboration (Syssner, 2016).

Box 3.4. Shrinking population: five types of policy responses

A traditional way to address population shrinkage at the regional and local government level has been the "going for growth" policy, in other words, to try to reverse shrinking trends and stimulate population growth (ESPON, 2017). However, a completely different approach has received a lot of attention recently. It has been argued by some researchers that a "coping with decline" strategy would form a more realistic way forward for declining population regions and municipalities. This strategy, also called "smart shrinking", means that shrinkage is accepted and the focus is on measures to adapt to its economic and social consequences (Haase, Hospers, Pekelsma, & Rink, 2012).

In practice, it is possible to identify five types of practical policy responses at the subnational level:

1. Trivialising shrinkage: situation where the local policymakers are presented demographic projections showing that the local jurisdiction will shrink in the coming years or decades. The data is however challenged by policymakers, leading to no response. This approach is likely to lead to budget deficits and indebtedness.

2. Countering shrinkage: policymakers define a strategy to counter shrinkage by attracting new residents and firms to the local jurisdiction. To be successful, this strategy requires realistic growth prospects and is likely to need strong financial support from the central government.

3. Accepting or managing shrinkage: policymakers actively define a strategy to improve the quality of life for the residents that decide to stay, instead of focusing on how to attract people from outside. It is perhaps the most realistic strategy, especially in a situation where the population has already declined for a long time and where there are no prospects for growth policy in the foreseeable future

4. Utilising shrinkage: policy that sees shrinking municipalities as societal laboratories where new methods are tested. The argument is that a municipality's quality of life does not depend on population density. This policy can work only if the local residents are able and willing to pay higher taxes for the local public services, or there is enough private service capacity to replace the public service provision.

5. Generalising shrinkage: combination of the "countering", "managing" and "utilising" approaches. In this alternative, reasonable growth prospects are utilised with support from the higher level of governments. In this policy alternative, it makes sense to focus more on current residents than on newcomers (Hospers & Reverda, 2015). The "generalising" policy is challenging from financing aspect and requires skilled local government management as well as active and engaged local decision-makers

Source: (OECD, forthcoming[11]), *Financing local public services and infrastructure in Estonia: challenges and ways forward*.

Recommendations

The mismatch between jurisdictions borders and the optimal public service benefit areas in Portugal affects the provision and delivery of public services in Alentejo. In the context of low population density, depopulation, and ageing, services can be redesigned in a manner that considers the functionality of the territory. In some cases, it is impossible for each entity to provide all services, rather, reorganising services delivery in a coordinated manner could improve access to services. Furthermore, financial constraints and the need for infrastructure call for more cooperation.

Alentejo could be a laboratory for using public policies to better align demographic trends with public service delivery. Regionalisation reforms, joint municipal authorities or formal co-operation between local governments, specific transfers from the central government could be used to better ensure that services are delivered efficiently and benefit all population.

Further pursuing decentralisation and regionalisation reforms to better align service provision and local needs

The regionalisation and decentralisation process may allow better serving the population. Decentralisation and regionalisation can spur accountability and good governance at the regional and local levels, in particular by aligning service provision to actual local needs. For this, Portugal needs to pursue regionalisation and decentralisation reforms. For this, key avenues are:

- At the local level, the transfer of competences to municipalities needs to be accompanied with the transfer of adequate financial resources as the capacity of municipalities to take over more responsibilities depend to a large extent on the transfer of resources. Incentives could be given to municipalities to take over more responsibilities, including receiving more fiscal resources (from grants) and powers (more own-source revenues). As a reference, Table 3.2 summarises the appropriate subnational government revenues for different expenditure categories. Beyond the transfer of resources it is important to ensure that municipalities have adequate human resources and equipment to undertake the new tasks that have been assigned.

Table 3.2 Appropriate subnational government revenue by category of expenditure

Service	Local taxes	User charges	Transfers	Borrowing
General administration	P	-	-	-
Education	P	S	P	(A)
Health	S	S	P	(A)
Welfare	S	-	P	-
Water supply	S	P*	-	A
Sewerage	S	P*	-	A
Drainage	P	P*	-	A
Markets and abattoirs	S	P*	-	(A)
Housing	S	P	S	A
Land development	-	P*	-	A
Streets	P	S*	-	A
Motorways	S	P*	P	A
Public transportation	S	P	-	A
Garbage collection	P	P	-	(A)
Garbage disposal	S	P	S	A
Parks and recreation	P	-	-	(A)
Fire protection	P	-	-	(A)
Police	P	-	-	-

Note: P= Primary source funding; S = Secondary source; A = Borrowing appropriate for major capital expenditures; (A) = Borrowing appropriate for capital expenditures but likely to account for a small share of spending. * = Development charges (special assessments, valorisation charges, etc.) are appropriate where benefits are spatially well defined within a jurisdiction. ** Transfers may be from regional or central government.
Source: Adapted and modified from (Bahl and Bird, 2018[12]), *Fiscal Decentralization and Local Finance in Developing Countries*, Edward Elgar Publishing, https://doi.org/10.4337/9781786435309.

- At the regional level, Alentejo could be a pilot region to organise the administration in a way that coincides with NUTS2. Alentejo could serve as a pilot to experiment a new model of regional governance. Within a country, there can be several forms of regionalisation depending on the challenges faced by the country and its particular needs. Different options are available (see Figure 3.11); one option would be, for example, to test the model of cooperative regions (association of municipalities at the regional TL2 level) as it is the case in Finland, Iceland, Ireland and Latvia. Across EU Member States and the OECD, regional associations of municipalities have different organisational structures, responsibilities and funding systems. The tasks of the co-operative regional governments are often limited to regional development and spatial planning, EU funds management and some other tasks with clear region-wide benefits such as environmental protection or regional roads. However, as an inter-municipal organisation, they can also execute tasks that are delegated by their members (e.g. waste collection or management of school offices in Iceland, and support co-operation and co-ordination between municipalities). They enjoy some decision-making autonomy on matters of regional jurisdiction. They have their own budget and are funded by municipal member fees. They can also receive central government transfers and EU funding. Co-operative regionalisation can be seen as an alternative to full regionalisation but also as an intermediate stage towards full regionalisation, such as in Finland and Latvia.

Figure 3.11. Four different models of regional organisation in the OECD and the EU

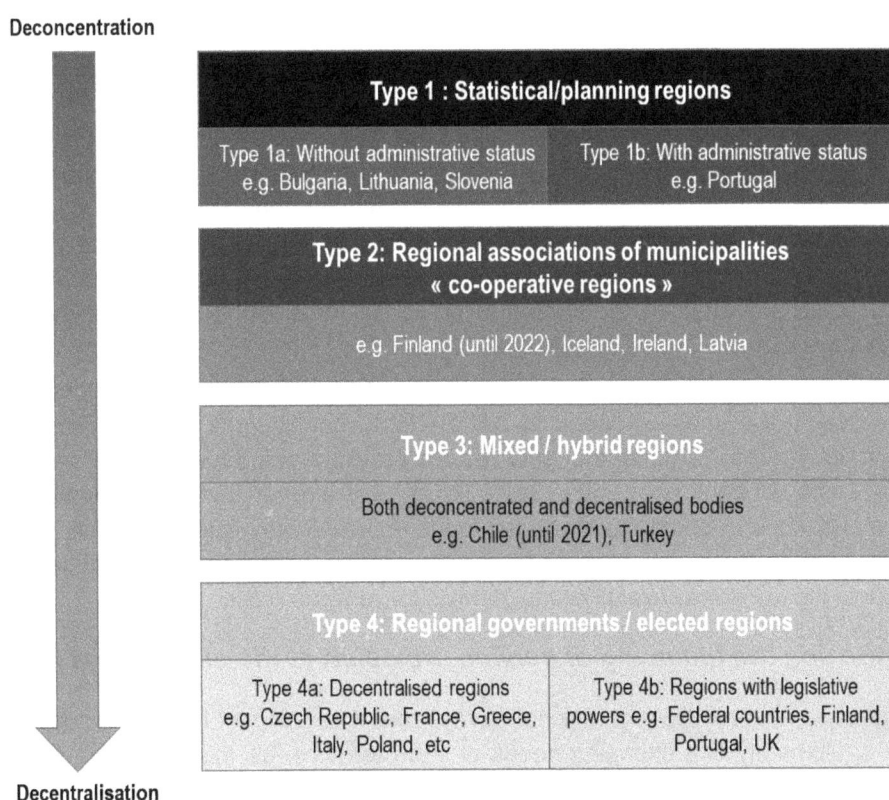

Source: (OECD, forthcoming[13]), *Regionalisation reforms in OECD countries and around the world.*

Encouraging cross-jurisdiction cooperation through concrete incentives

Further encouraging inter-municipal association to provide decentralised services could improve service provision in education, health care and social support. The central government needs to adopt a proactive role in promoting and stimulating inter-municipal cooperation in the provision of decentralised services.

Municipalities are stronger and more competitive when they join forces and take advantage of economies of scale. IMCs are also better positioned to identify investment and relevant actions with supra-municipal benefits. To encourage collaboration the following actions could be beneficial:

- The central government could accelerate the process of inter-municipal cooperation with financial incentives. To stimulate collaboration among municipalities, it is helpful to design programmes fostering cooperation rather than competition across jurisdictions. One way to accomplish this could be to use the transfer system, for example by directing more transfers to IMCs, instead of municipalities, particularly with respect to public services with important externalities (OECD, 2020[11]). Along the same lines, EU funds could be directed to inter-municipal projects conducted by inter-municipal communities.

- Build on already successful inter-municipal co-operation mechanisms in the region (or in other regions in Portugal) and to adopt a strategy to actively promote them and encourage peer-learning.

- Leverage inter-municipal companies for the delivery of basic services at the inter-municipal level could also bring important benefits, as it is the case of the water utility company and a waste treatment company in Lezíria do Tejo. Further developing joint-procurement might be also useful to reduce costs as scale increases, for instance to finance telecommunications and school meals.

- Fostering technical capacity through cooperation among parishes could enable them to effectively perform their tasks and deliver local services to residents. Parishes can play an important role in articulating service delivery in very low-density areas. In some cases, however, parishes would benefit from cooperating with adjacent parishes in another municipality. Cross-jurisdiction cooperation could even extend to cross-border. For example, in the case of the municipality of Barrancos and its surroundings, cross-border co-operation could increase service quality to the level of Elvas' and lower territorial disparities in access and use of public services.

- Take better advantage of the conditions established by the current regulatory framework on IMCs for Alentejo to explore instances of co-operation with neighbouring regions and knowledge sharing with regions that face similar problems. This would permit Alentejo to take advantage of peer experiences in facing the challenges brought by a shrinking and ageing population. This peer learning, while promoted by the central level, could, for example, be conducted with regions in Spain that are currently facing similar challenges.

- Identify municipalities or groups of municipalities pertaining to the same functional area– which are not necessarily the ones grouped in IMCs - that could benefit the most from scaling-up the provision of services. Ensuring that services are provided at the functional allows benefitting from spill-overs and economies of scale. Some IMCs have already started to develop maps of public services and this task should be extended to the entire Alentejo's territory. This mapping needs to identify which services may benefit from joint-provision considering functional areas, and not necessarily the administrative divisions of IMCs currently in place.

Strengthening the financing of service provision at the subnational level

Current fiscal arrangements in Portugal do not always take into account territorial, social and economic specificities, and, ultimately, the changing needs of each territory resulting from demographic changes. This means that many municipalities in Alentejo especially those that are smaller and scarcely populated –and which are ultimately the most affected by the demographic challenge-, face large difficulties in providing access to quality services in a sustainable way. Fiscal arrangements need to be gradually reformed in order to ensure that municipalities will still be able to properly finance service provision and ensure citizen's well-being over time. For this, some of the measures that could be taken are the following:

- Strengthening the municipal own revenue base in a gradual manner. A high reliance on transfers and a low taxing power may have a negative effect on the efficiency of municipal service delivery. This can be done by exploring the possibility of increasing the leverage that municipalities have on to tax rates (i.e. on the Property Tax and the Surcharge Tax), and the proportion of the personal income tax that stays with municipalities. With this, municipalities can make a more efficient use of these instruments to attract people and investments. This needs to be accompanied with proper accountability measures so that citizens have a clear idea which are the taxes that are managed by municipalities.

- Guarantee financial means of IMCs to particularly benefit small municipalities that have less capacity to raise own revenues. IMCs currently receive only a marginal amount of transfers (0.5% of the FEF) and have a very restricted capacity to raise own revenues. To enlarge the role of IMCs and make them less dependent on the municipal will of delegating task, it would be important to increase the amount of transfers. This increment can be subject to particular outputs that can be previously defined between the central level and the concerned IMCs (see above).

References

ANMP (2021), *Associations of Special Purpose Municipalities*, https://www.anmp.pt/municipios/associacoes-de-municipios-de-fins-especificos/ (accessed on 2021). [7]

Bahl, R. and R. Bird (2018), *Fiscal Decentralization and Local Finance in Developing Countries*, Edward Elgar Publishing, https://doi.org/10.4337/9781786435309. [12]

CCDR Alentejo (2020), *Alentejo 2030: regional strategy*, https://www.ccdr-a.gov.pt/docs/ccdra/gestao/ER2030.pdf. [2]

CCDR-A (2021), *Comissão de Coordenação e Desenvolvimento Regional do Alentejo*, https://www.ccdr-a.gov.pt/. [3]

DGAL (2021), *Regime financeiro das autarquias locais*, http://www.portalautarquico.dgal.gov.pt/pt-PT/financas-locais/ (accessed on 30 October 2021). [10]

Eurostat (2021), *General government expenditure by function (COFOG)*, https://ec.europa.eu/eurostat/databrowser/view/GOV_10A_EXP/default/table?lang=en (accessed on 30 October 2021). [4]

Forum das Cidades (2020), *Pacts for Development and Territorial Cohesion*, https://www.forumdascidades.pt/content/pactos-para-o-desenvolvimento-e-coesao-territorial. [6]

OECD (2021), *Subnational governments in OECD countries: key data*, https://stats.oecd.org/Index.aspx?DataSetCode=SNGF. [9]

OECD (2020), *Decentralisation and Regionalisation in Portugal*, OECD, https://doi.org/10.1787/fea62108-en (accessed on May 2021). [1]

OECD (2017), *Multi-level Governance Reforms: Overview of OECD Country Experiences*, OECD Publishing. [8]

OECD (forthcoming), *Financing local public services and infrastructure in Estonia: challenges and ways forward*. [11]

OECD (forthcoming), *Regionalisation reforms in OECD countries and around the world*. [13]

OECD-UCLG (2019), *World Observatory on Subnational Government Finance and Investment*, https://www.sng-wofi.org/. [5]

4 Forward-looking planning for the provision of basic education

Introduction

In 2005, an ambitious school consolidation reform in Portugal aimed to address the school network's inefficiency and strong regional inequalities. The reform accomplished the goal of reducing the number of redundant schools – mostly located in rural areas – and increase efficiency. While school consolidation is efficiency-enhancing, it may lead to increased school transportation times and costs in remote and sparsely populated areas.

School transportation is one of the main concerns of Alentejo rural inhabitants, especially for young children and those living in the lower part of Alentejo. Students face the challenges of long travel distances and significant time of travel, of over an hour in many cases, leading them to wake up at early hours of the morning. This negatively affects their learning experience and represents a serious educational equity problem.

At the same time, the issue of access to school varies with the level of local capacity to deal with the issue, so large inequalities in access across Alentejo are linked not only to geographical and demographic differences but also by the way local transport is organised. As explained in previous chapters, Portugal has a partial decentralisation model that has resulted in a mixed responsibility model, where the national government is mostly responsible for the managing of the school network and the teaching body, and municipalities are responsible for the provision and financing of school transport.

This chapter analyses the trade-off between cost-efficiency, access, and quality faced by rural municipalities in Alentejo. The first section discusses the main features of the national and regional educational system, including recent decentralisation reforms. The second section analyses cost, access and quality statistics for Alentejo at different levels of aggregation (TL3, municipality and degree of urbanisation), including foresight analysis based on simulated placement of schools. Finally, the last section presents seven policy recommendations for Alentejo's consideration, summarised in the following box.

Recommendations on forward-looking planning for the provision of basic education

The current chapter suggests recommendations on the provision of basic education detailed in the Recommendations section:

Taking into account the effects of demographic change is necessary to bridge the quality and access gaps and improve the restructuring and planning of the school network

- Design a specific strategy to bridge quality and access gaps in lagging and remote rural municipalities
- Use educational charters to coordinate actions among neighbouring municipalities
- Encourage multi-level cooperation towards innovative models including service co-location, and plan strategically the location of new schools based on future demand projections

Achieving better quality education also requires improving the geographic mobility of teachers while increasing within school efficiency

- Revise the national model of teaching recruitment to include the participation of municipalities and regional authorities in the process
- Enhance geographic mobility of teachers (especially young ones)

Increased efforts are needed to bridge the digital divide and enhance the digitalisation of public services to overcome the challenges of school transport

- Further develop transport on demand solutions
- Increase cooperation between municipalities for the provision of transport
- Create a committee of volunteer teachers at the regional level to support teachers from rural communities with the most difficulties in their adaptation and training process
- Support networks bringing together employees from digital sectors and teachers

Establishing a strategy for student accommodation could contribute to solve the challenges of school transport

- Support the accommodation of students over 16 years of age during school days
- Restructure the network of student residences in order to better match supply with demand efficiently

Main features of the national and regional education system

The Portuguese educational system has undergone several reforms in the past decades, mostly related to the clustering of small schools, the decentralisation of education responsibilities from the national government to municipalities or its digitalisation. This section discusses the main features of the national education system and the trends in students, teachers and schools in Alentejo in the last decade.

National system

The basic compulsory education system in Portugal comprises 12 years of education between the ages of 6 and 18 (or completion of secondary education). The compulsory school network is organised in two levels: basic education (1ˢᵗ, 2ⁿᵈ and 3ʳᵈ cycle) and secondary education[1]The Ministry of Education is responsible for managing the public school network at all levels (pre-school to secondary education).

Since the 2005 reform, the school network is organised into school clusters of an average of 4-7 schools composed of pre-school establishments plus one or more teaching levels and cycles with a common pedagogical project, covering 98% of all primary, lower secondary and upper secondary public schools (Liebowitz et al., 2018[1]). Within a decade, the 2005 consolidation reform resulted in the closure of 47% of the country's public schools (5 600 schools). In parallel, municipalities also participated in the reorganization of 1ˢᵗ cycle school network, leading to the closure of thousands of schools (Liebowitz et al., 2018[2]). The drop in the number of public schools and kindergartens was especially pronounced in the period 2010-2015 (8 351 to 5 834 schools) and slowed down afterwards to reach 5 373 schools in 2020/21.

School clusters have their own administration and management bodies and retain some autonomy in pedagogy and curriculum management under the guidelines of the Ministry of Education. The 2016 National Programme for the Promotion of School Success (*Programa Nacional de Promoção do Sucesso Escolar - PNPSE*) (PNPSE/ DGE, 2019[3]) pursued a territorial, bottom-up and co-responsibility approach of the programme to decentralise competences to municipalities (equipment, supporting services, extracurricular activities) and fostering of partnerships between schools and local entities (bookshops, sports clubs, health centres, etc.) (Diário da República, 2016[4]).

Two recent decrees aimed at extending the autonomy of school clusters and promote decentralisation by assigning responsibilities to municipalities regarding investment, equipment and the maintenance of school buildings, the provision of meals in establishments and management of non-teaching staff, social support programmes, prevention of school failure and early leaving projects, among others.[2] However, decisions related to teaching staff, such as hiring or firing and compensation, remain the sole responsibility of the Ministry of Education.

The partial decentralisation of education services also means that decisions on schools opening or closures are coordinated between national and local authorities. Specifically, the national government adjusts the public school network every year based on proposals from municipalities and a diagnosis of the network carried out by the regional education authorities that includes the expected number of students in each school. A previous directive from 2010 that based school closures on an absolute threshold (21 students) has been replaced by consideration for closure based on the number of students in pre-schooling (5 children) or primary schools (10 children) if there is another school in a given perimeter (5 km for pre-schooling and 10 km for primary).

While school closures are the main competence of the Ministry of Education, support for travel costs including for students affected by school closures is a competence of municipalities (except in the case of special needs students which are covered by national authorities).[3]

Finally, Portugal has launched several strategies and initiatives in recent years to accelerate the digitalisation of its education system and to promote distance learning (Box 4.1). The various reforms have mainly focused on improving Internet connectivity, digital resources and technological equipment in schools, as well as strengthening the digital skills of students, teachers and parents.

The 2020 Action Plan for Digital Transition called "Portugal Digital" includes the Digitalisation Program for Schools that aims to improve the equipment, resources, and connectivity in Portugal's schools. The programme seeks to stimulate creativity and innovation through digitalisation in the teaching-learning process and to provide quality distance learning and online collaborative work. It also involves a digital training plan for teachers to ensure the acquisition of the necessary skills for teaching in the new digital context, with the objective to reach 100% of teachers with digital skills by 2023 (Government of Portugal, 2020[5]). Teachers can evaluate their level of digital competence through the European online self-assessment tool (TET-SAT), which is available in all Portugal's schools (European Commission/EACEA/Eurydice, 2019[6]). "Portugal Digital" also includes a plan on interactive digital educational resources, with a pilot project on the use of digital textbooks (*Projeto-Piloto de Desmaterialização de Manuais Escolares*).

In parallel, the 2017 National Digital Skills Initiative 2030 (or "Portugal INCoDe.2030") promotes digital skills among teachers and students in a timeframe that goes from 2018 until 2030. This initiative includes the training of teacher trainers who will subsequently develop the digital skills of the approximately 100 000 primary and secondary school teachers in the Portuguese educational system. The goal of these "Digital Ambassadors" is also to boost the implementation of local digital transition plans from the Training Centres (*Centros de Formação de Associação de Escolas*). Through "Portugal INCoDe.2030", the country has adopted a new and progressive curriculum framework introducing Information and Communication Technologies (ICT) and digital competences in all basic stages of education. Teaching digital skills is cross-curricular in lower primary education (grades 1-4) while in upper primary (grades 5-6) and lower secondary education, ICT is a compulsory separate subject. In upper secondary education, ICT is an optional separate subject. The introduction of this new subject has been done progressively over several phases: in the 2018-2019 school year, the reform took place only in the first years of each cycle (grades 1, 5 and 7); in the 2019-2020 school year, the reform was gradually extended to grades 2, 6 and 8; in 2020-2021, to grades 3 and 9; and in 2021-2022, to grade 4.

Finally, the Ministry of Education has launched many other initiatives to strengthen the digitalisation of education, including some to improve technological equipment in classrooms (*Operação Computadores na Sala de Aula*; *Operação Escola Interativa*; *Kit Tecnológico nas Escolas Secundárias*), to centralise information on the education and training offer in Portugal (*Portal Oferta Formativa*), or to improve parents' technology skills (*Academia Digital para Pais*). Regarding this last initiative, the Digital Academy Programme for Parents gives the opportunity to parents or guardians of 1st and 2nd cycle children from Educational Territories of Priority Intervention Programme (TEIP) schools to attend training courses that promote digital skills. In Alentejo, the programme has been developed in six school clusters TEIP (Direção-Geral da Educação, n.d.[7]).

Source: (Government of Portugal, 2020[5]), Plano de Ação para a Transição Digital de Portugal, https://www.portugal.gov.pt/gc22/portugal-digital/plano-de-acao-para-a-transicao-digital-pdf.aspx ; (European Commission/EACEA/Eurydice, 2019[6]), Digital Education at School in Europe, Eurydice Report, Luxembourg: Publications Office of the European Union, https://eacea.ec.europa.eu/national-policies/eurydice/sites/default/files/en_digital_education_n.pdf ; (Direção-Geral da Educação, n.d.[7]), Academia Digital para Pais, https://www.dge.mec.pt/academia-digital-para-pais

Educational system in Alentejo

While the number of primary school students decreased between 2009 and 2019, both teachers and schools decreased at a faster pace as a result of the consolidation process (Table 4.1). Within Alentejo, Alentejo Litoral had the largest difference between student and school change rates (10 percentage points), followed by Lezíria do Tejo (9 percentage points). In secondary education, the rate of decrease of teachers and schools was slower than the decrease in the number of students, as expected from the higher specialisation in the education offer in upper higher education and the larger size of secondary schools.

Even after school consolidation, in 2019 all municipalities in Alentejo had at least one primary and one lower secondary school. Out of 58 municipalities, 8 had only one primary school and 28 had only one lower secondary school, 4 more than in 2009. Upper secondary provision is more concentrated in space as a result of previous consolidation: in 2019, 10 municipalities did not have an upper secondary school, up from 9 municipalities in 2009.

The number of primary schools decreased in 47 out of 58 municipalities in 2009-2019, with changes ranging from 1 to 51 less schools. A substantial part of the consolidation of the school network involved small schools in rural areas. In Alentejo, the number of schools with less than 21 students dropped from around 100 before 2014 to around 30, with a few cases of municipalities with more than one small school, including Santiago do Cacém with 4 small schools, Évora with 3, and Almodôvar, Alcácer do Sal, Serpa, Elvas and Montemor-o-Novo with 2 schools each.

Table 4.1. Evolution on number of schools, students and teachers in Alentejo

2009-2019

	2009	2019	Change	2009	2019	Change
	Primary			Secondary		
Schools						
Alentejo Litoral	85	67	-21%	28	27	-4%
Baixo Alentejo	115	90	-22%	48	45	-6%
Lezíria do Tejo	187	136	-27%	52	53	2%
Alto Alentejo	99	76	-23%	40	35	-13%
Alentejo Central	141	101	-28%	45	44	-2%
Total Alentejo	**627**	**470**	**-25%**	**213**	**204**	**-4%**
Students						
Alentejo Litoral	5 861	5 234	-11%	8 810	5 947	-32%
Baixo Alentejo	8 486	7 057	-17%	12 687	8 202	-35%
Lezíria do Tejo	17 103	13 913	-19%	20 800	16 370	-21%
Alto Alentejo	7 585	5 869	-23%	11 025	7 227	-34%
Alentejo Central	10 964	8 531	-22%	16 869	10 515	-38%
Total Alentejo	**49 999**	**40 604**	**-19%**	**70 191**	**48 261**	**-31%**
Teachers						
Alentejo Litoral	576	482	-16%	814	612	-25%
Baixo Alentejo	869	713	-18%	1 107	859	-22%
Lezíria do Tejo	1 537	1 219	-21%	1 812	1 630	-10%
Alto Alentejo	766	628	-18%	1 064	902	-15%
Alentejo Central	1 048	794	-24%	1 512	1 230	-19%
Total Alentejo	**4 796**	**3 836**	**-20%**	**6 309**	**5 233**	**-17%**

Source: (PORTDATA, 2021[8]).

Cost, access and quality of education in Alentejo

The provision of educational services in rural areas involves a trade-off between cost-efficiency, quality and access (OECD, 2021[9]). In Alentejo, these trade-offs are particularly evident in sparsely populated, small and remote municipalities that face at the same time high costs, long distances and lower quality. This section evaluates the status of each dimension based on national statistics and cost and access estimates. It offers a comparative picture across TL3 regions, municipalities and degrees of urbanisation in Alentejo to assess the level of territorial inequalities. The section finalises with a foresight analysis based on different policy scenarios with a 2035 horizon.

Alentejo has both top and bottom performing regions in education quality

Regarding quality, PISA 2018 test results show strong variations within Alentejo. While Alentejo Central consistently performs above the national average across TL3 regions in both scores, Alto and Baixo Alentejo have the lowest scores. Moreover, while both regions have smaller shares of top performers and larger shares of low performers, these shares are in line with national averages in Alentejo Central. Analysis at the national level has also shown a rural-urban gap in performance, which nevertheless disappears after controlling for socio-economic status of the students (OECD, 2021[9]).

Table 4.2. Student performance means by TL3 region in Alentejo

PISA 2018 test

	PISA reading score average (s.d. in parenthesis)	PISA maths score average (s.d. in parenthesis)	PISA science score average (s.d. in parenthesis)	Top performers in science (%)	Low performers in science (%)
Alentejo Litoral	462 (11,1)	464 (13,8)	463 (11,8)	3.5	28.2
Lezíria do Tejo	479 (10,1)	478 (9,4)	483 (11,7)	4.4	25
Alto Alentejo	446 (22,9)	444 (17,7)	450 (17,1)	2.1	33.9
Alentejo Central	492 (12,7)	497 (13,8)	495 (13,6)	5.6	19.7
Baixo Alentejo	448 (14,8)	451 (12,0)	443 (13,2)	3.1	40.6
Portugal	492 (2,4)	492 (2,7)	492 (2,8)	5.6	19.6

Note: s.d. = standard deviation
Source: (Instituto de Avaliação Educativa IP, 2019[10]) and (OECD, 2020[11])

Portugal has long struggled with another indicator of education quality: retention and dropout rates.[4] The country made substantial progress over the last decade to reduce its high share of early school leavers and Alentejo was not the exception. As Table 4.3 shows, the region had retention and dropout rates close to the national average in 2019. Additionally, all TL3 regions managed to reduce retention and dropout rates between 2009-2019, even substantially in the case of high initial rates in the 2nd and 3rd cycles of basic education (i.e., in the 10-14 age range). However, the gap with respect to the regional average for the 3rd cycle widened in Alentejo Central and especially Baixo Alentejo, as both regions failed to improve their retention and dropout rates at the same pace as other regions.

Table 4.3. Retention and dropout rates in basic education by TL3 regions in Alentejo

Percentage of enrolled students in grades 1-9 who failed or dropped out by basic education cycle

	Basic education (1st cycle)		Basic education (2nd cycle)		Basic education (3rd cycle)	
	2009	2019	2009	2019	2009	2019
Lezíria do Tejo	4.1%	2.5%	9.4%	4.7%	13.1%	4.4%
Alto Alentejo	3.7%	3.2%	7.8%	6.7%	9.1%	4.4%
Alentejo Litoral	4.0%	1.7%	11.1%	3.2%	13.1%	5.2%
Alentejo Central	3.8%	2.5%	8.3%	5.1%	11.9%	6.9%
Baixo Alentejo	4.8%	5.3%	10.1%	7.3%	15.8%	8.9%
Alentejo	4.1%	3.0%	9.2%	5.3%	12.6%	5.8%
Portugal	3.6%	2.1%	7.6%	3.8%	14.0%	5.8%

Source: (PORTDATA, 2021[8])

The reduction in retention and dropout rates in the past years happened in the context of a PNPSE program at the end of the 2015/2016 school year. The program requested school clusters and ungrouped schools to design strategic action plans to be implemented in the following two school years (PNPSE/ DGE, 2019[3]). In the context of the implementation of the programme, Alto Alentejo was one of three TL3 regions in Portugal where more than 60% of schools managed to reduce retention in the 1st, 2nd and 3rd cycles by at least 25% (Figure 4.1). The other four TL3 regions of Alentejo, however, saw slower progress, especially Baixo Alentejo where only 25% of schools managed to reduce retention in the 2nd cycle by at least 25%. On the other hand, Alentejo Central had considerable differences between cycles: 67% of schools managed to improve their retention rates by at least 25% in the 1st cycle and only 23% of schools achieved the same improvement in the 3rd cycle.

Figure 4.1. Relative shares (%) of schools per TL3 region that have reduced their retention and dropout rates by at least 25%, in each education cycle, between the 2014-2016 biennium and the 2016-18 biennium

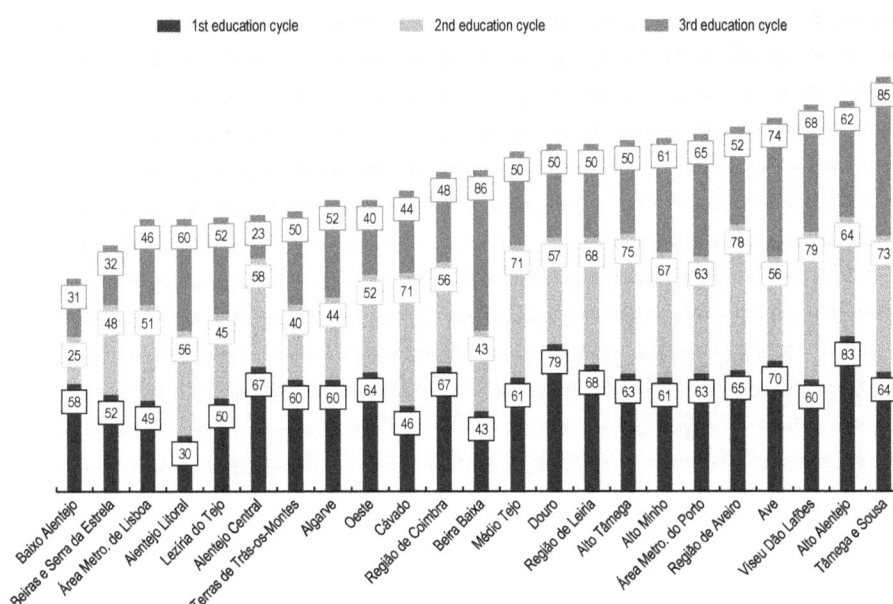

Note: Data from Direção-Geral de Estatísticas da Educação e Ciência (DGEEC). Região Autónoma dos Açores and Região Autónoma da Madeira are not represented in the Figure.
Source: (PNPSE/ DGE, 2019[3])

The large improvement made by some TL3 regions despite high initial levels suggest that school success depends largely on the pedagogical, didactic and organisational measures undertaken by schools and municipalities under the right incentive schemes. On the other hand, the differences across educational levels suggest that teaching cultures according to the cycles of basic education have an impact on results (PNPSE/ DGE, 2019[3]). Nevertheless, the widening gaps between Baixo Alentejo and Alentejo Central vis-à-vis the rest of the regions suggests that geographic and demographic factors may be also at play.

Efficiency within schools has improved but remains below OECD levels

Expenditure by student data is not systematically calculated at any geographical level in Portugal, according to the responses from relevant authorities to the OECD study survey. Available data for 2014 shows that expenditure per student in Portugal is below OECD levels in all educational levels, which is expected given lower teacher wages in Portugal compared to the OECD mean (Liebowitz et al., 2018[2]) (OECD, 2021[9]). The country actually spends a larger proportion of its GDP in all basic educational levels (in primary 1.8% versus 1.5%, in lower secondary 1.3% versus 1.0% and in upper secondary 1.4% versus 1.2%) and spends 33% more in secondary education compared to primary.

In absence of expenditure data, statistics on teacher-to-school ratios can give an idea about within school efficiency. In 2019 there were on average about 10.6 students per teacher in primary schools and 9.2 students per teacher in secondary schools in Alentejo, in line with national values and below the OECD average of 13 and 12 students per teacher (OECD, 2021[9]). Available data for primary schools in 2017/2018 shows that, similar to the national level, average student-to-teacher ratios across schools in Alentejo are lowest in villages (10.8), followed by sparse rural areas (11.3) and towns and suburbs (14), although the ratio varies more widely in this last category (standard deviation of 11 compared to 4-5 in sparse rural areas and villages).

Student-to-teacher ratios in primary schools increased between 2009 and 2015 and then decreased in 2015-2019. This reverse in trend happened in both urban municipalities such as Benavente, Vendas Novas and Évora that had a larger ratio to start with and in smaller rural municipalities that had the lowest ratios (i.e. 4-5 students per teacher below the regional mean) (Figure 4.2). Meanwhile, average student-to-teacher ratios in secondary schools remained stable.

Figure 4.2. Highest and lowest student-to-teacher ratio evolution by municipalities in Alentejo

2009-2019

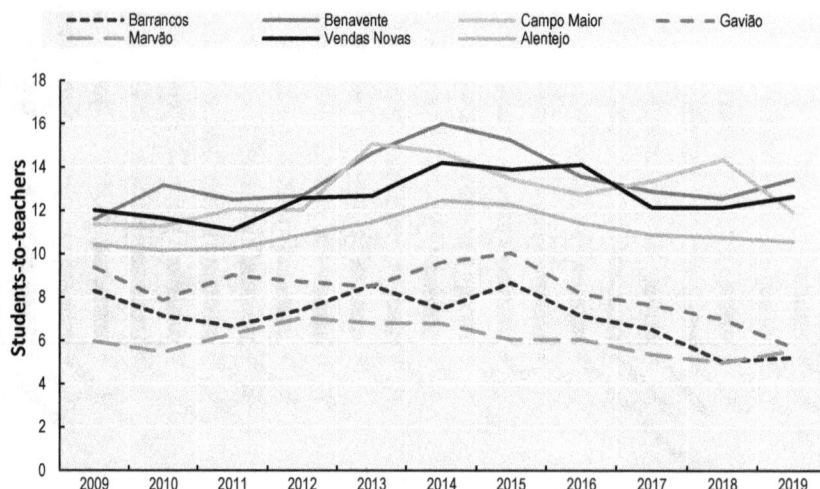

Source: (PORTDATA, 2021[8]).

Long travel to school times and costs affect the motivation of students and teachers in remote areas

Many times, school and buses schedules are not compatible, especially in the afternoon's way back. On the other hand, during weekends and school holidays, school transport is much scarcer or even inexistent during the summer holidays. This prevents many children from leaving their municipalities for extra-curricular activities offered by other schools during these periods.

In secondary education, the low diversity of educational provision in rural areas and long travel times may be behind high retention and dropout rates as well as demotivation rates. Many rural small localities offer only one programme of study, which prevents students with limited access to transport from choosing the programme they are most interested in according to their academic and professional goals. This is also true for vocational education. As students enrol in the only vocational training course offered by their municipality, they may lack of motivation because it is not their first choice.

At the same time, long travel distances between facilities are of concern for teachers in the most remote schools of Alentejo. Given the absence of public transport alternatives, teachers have to spend a significant part of their day driving to school locations. Analysis from the mission study found that some teachers experience demotivation and high stress levels from having to travel long distances to reach schools as part of their work in clustered rural schools.

Cost and distance estimates reveal a tight trade-offs for many rural municipalities

This sub-section reviews evidence on costs and access estimations based on school location simulation and actual demand produced by (OECD/EC-JRC, 2021[12]). "Costs" include running costs such as salaries and ICT equipment, and exclude capital or fixed investments such as school building construction or renovation. The excess of cost in a region results mostly from the presence of small schools in areas with low local demand, and can be interpreted as a measure of the unavoidable costs of smallness and remoteness. Costs are measured at the place of residency of students, so when aggregated they are meant to capture the situation experienced by students living in a municipality regardless of whether they attend school within the municipal borders or not.

According to the estimates, annual costs per primary and secondary student in Alentejo were 10% and 6%-7% above the average for Portugal and EU27+UK. All TL3 regions in Alentejo, except for Lezíria do Tejo, are on the top 10% highest primary and secondary costs per student across EU27+UK regions (Table 4.4). Regions with higher costs also have smaller share of kids and adolescents in school age, with a difference of almost two percentage points between the region with the lowest and highest shares (Alentejo Litoral versus Lezíria do Tejo). The share of 5-19 year-olds across TL3 regions in Alentejo is also lower (13%-15%) compared to the average for remote regions across EU27+UK regions (16%).

Table 4.4. Rank of annual cost per student among EU27+UK TL3 regions and share of 5-19 year-olds

Percentile rank from smallest to highest annual costs across 1 348 EU27+UK regions (100% = highest value across OECD regions)

TL3 region	Rank annual primary school costs per student, 2011 (%)	Rank annual secondary school costs per student, 2011 (%)	Share 5 to 19 year-olds in total population (%)
Alentejo Litoral	97%	98%	13.0%
Baixo Alentejo	96%	98%	13.9%

Alto Alentejo	94%	94%	13.7%
Alentejo Central	92%	93%	14.0%
Lezíria do Tejo	67%	74%	14.9%

Source: Author's elaboration based on (OECD/EC-JRC, 2021[12]).

Both cost and distances per student vary widely across municipalities in Alentejo, and some clearly face both high cost and high distances. Distance per student estimates across municipalities reveal a high dispersion in travel times that are even wider across schools. For primary schools, distances vary between less than 1km to over 4km, while for secondary schools distances range between less than 3km to over 12km (Figure 4.3). At the school level, distances to primary and secondary schools can go above 9km and 18km and costs can exceed EUR 10 000 and EUR 8 500 in the smallest and most remote municipalities. Some municipalities where there is a relatively larger proportion of students in primary school age, including all municipalities in Lezíria do Tejo, have relatively small costs but widely varying distances for primary schools. In contrast, many municipalities face both high costs and high distances. The most extreme case is Mértola, a municipality near the Spanish border of about 7 000 inhabitants that had 4 times less people in 2011 compared to 1960.

Figure 4.3. Annual costs and distance per student by municipality

2011

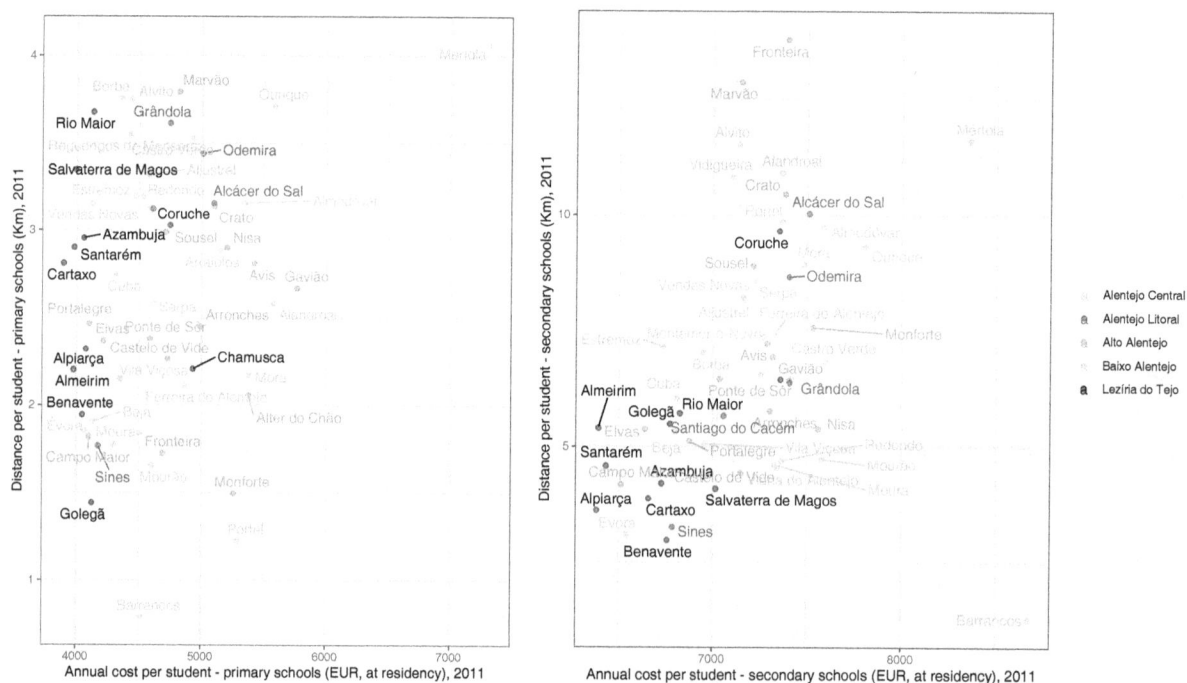

Source: Author's elaboration based on (OECD/EC-JRC, 2021[12]).

Many municipalities that face high distances and costs also have higher retention and dropout rates

The comparison of actual and simulated indicators by municipality can reveal differences between the actual school network to one resulting from an efficient allocation of students (i.e., one based on transport cost minimisation under no administrative limitations on catchment areas). The comparison is and is made in relative terms to account for absolute differences in the number of students across municipalities stemming from the different student population considered.[5]

Figure 4.4 plots the actual minus simulated number of students per school against the actual minus simulated number of students per teacher by municipality. These variables aim to capture differences in the level of spatial concentration and within school efficiency compared to the benchmark case. Out of the 58 municipalities in Alentejo, 16 are on the lower right quadrant of the graph, indicating that those municipalities may have higher average efficiency and spatial concentration compared to the simulated placement. While data availability does not allow corroboration, it is likely that students in those municipalities travel longer distances to schools compared to what the simulated placement predicts.

Figure 4.4. Actual versus simulated students per school and students per teacher by municipality

2011

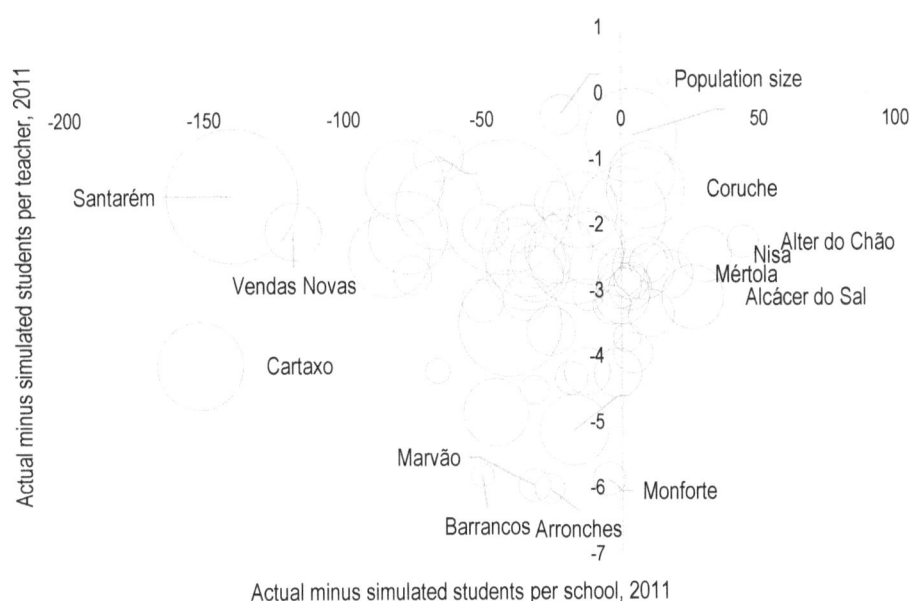

Actual minus simulated students per school, 2011

Source: Author's elaboration based on (OECD/EC-JRC, 2021[12]) and (PORTDATA, 2021[8]).

To generally evaluate if there is a relationship between costs and access on the one hand, and quality indicators on the other, Figure 4.5 plots actual retention and dropout rates in lower secondary (3rd cycle) by municipality against estimates of annual costs and distances for secondary schools. Generally, municipalities that have higher distances and costs also show higher retention and dropout rates. This is especially evident in Ourique and Vidigueira in Baixo Alentejo and Mora in Alentejo Central. The small size of schools and how difficult they are to reach may be discouraging students from continuing their studies.

Figure 4.5. Annual cost and distance per student versus retention and dropout rates by municipalities (secondary)

2011 and 2019

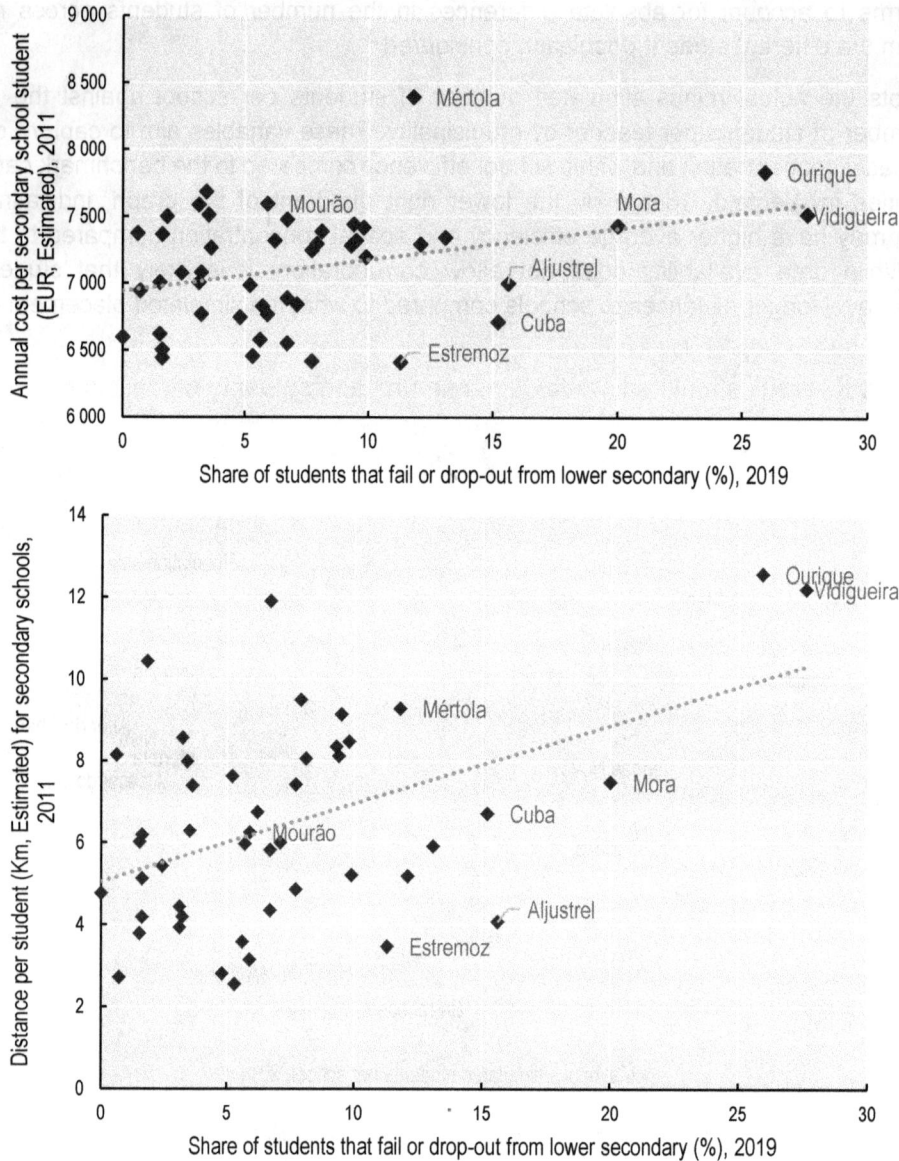

Source: Author's elaboration based on (OECD/EC-JRC, 2021[12]) and (PORTDATA, 2021[8]).

Future policy scenarios by degree of urbanisation

After establishing cost, quality and access trade-offs, this section focuses on future policy scenarios for Alentejo. Data across degrees of urbanisation reveals that both cost and distance per student are higher in sparse rural areas, that in 2011 concentrated 27% of primary school and 12% of secondary school students (Table 4.5). By 2035, the number of primary and secondary students is projected to decrease by 29% and 26%, with stronger declines projected in towns and suburbs (37% and 27%).

Table 4.5 summarises key indicators under two different scenarios: 1) what if the school network in 2035 responded efficiently to new demand levels? (i.e. the school network to 2035 is set up according to 2035 student numbers or "2035 students/2035 schools" scenario) and 2) what if the present school network is kept intact in the future? (i.e. keeping the same 2011 school network in 2035 or "2035 students/2011 schools" scenario). Under the first scenario:

- the number of primary schools would decrease by 10%, with the largest changes concentrated in towns and suburbs (20 out of 39 schools less);
- the number of secondary schools would decrease by 18%, with the largest changes concentrated in villages (11 out of 24 schools less);
- The percentage change in number of teachers in primary and secondary schools would roughly correspond to the decrease in the number of students, except for proportionally higher decreases in sparse rural areas for the case of secondary schools;
- Annual costs per student in primary and secondary schools would increase 4% and 1%, while distances per student would change slightly, with the largest changes in villages for the case of secondary schools;
- Adapting the school network to future demand would create significant changes in remote areas, despite low average changes (Figure 4.6).

In contrast, under the second scenario:

- The number of teachers in primary schools would decrease more than proportionally than the drop in the number of students in sparse rural areas and villages, and less than proportionally in towns and suburbs. Compared to the first scenario, this represents a drop of around 663 instead of 715 teachers in sparse rural areas and 745 instead of 769 teachers in villages, and 913 instead of 846 in towns an suburbs;
- The number of teachers in primary schools would decrease more than proportionally than the drop in the number of students in all areas, with the largest differences in sparse rural areas;
- Annual cost per student in primary schools would increase more than under the first scenario, especially in towns and suburbs, while distances would decrease slightly. On the other hand, costs and distances per student for secondary schools would remain roughly similar compared to the initial situation.

Table 4.5. Summary of changes in key cost and access indicators by degree of urbanisation

2011-2035

Degree of urbanisation	2011			2011-2035	2035 students/2035 schools				2035 students/2011 schools		
	Share of students (%)	Annual costs per student rel. to min. (%)	Distance per student (Km)	Change in students (%)	Change in schools (%)	Change in teachers (%)	Change in annual costs per student (%)	Change in distance (Km)	Change in teachers (%)	Change in annual costs per student (%)	Change in distance (Km)
Primary schools											
Sparse rural	27%	31%	4.72	-22%	-8%	-22%	4%	0.12	-28%	1%	-0.14
Villages	31%	13%	2.11	-24%	-3%	-25%	5%	0.09	-27%	3%	-0.12
Towns and suburbs	43%	0%	1.70	-37%	-29%	-37%	1%	-0.05	-32%	12%	-0.05
Total	100%			-29%	-10%	-29%	4%		-30%	6%	
Secondary schools											

Sparse rural	12%	16%	11.53	-21%	-20%	-23%	-1%	-0.45	-26%	-2%	0.07
Villages	42%	11%	6.99	-26%	-16%	-27%	0%	0.91	-28%	0%	-0.10
Towns and suburbs	46%	0%	3.24	-27%	-19%	-26%	2%	0.12	-28%	1%	-0.06
Total	100%			-26%	-18%	-26%	1%		-28%	0%	

Source: Author's elaboration based on (OECD/EC-JRC, 2021[12])

Figure 4.6. Projected change in distance to primary schools

2011-2035

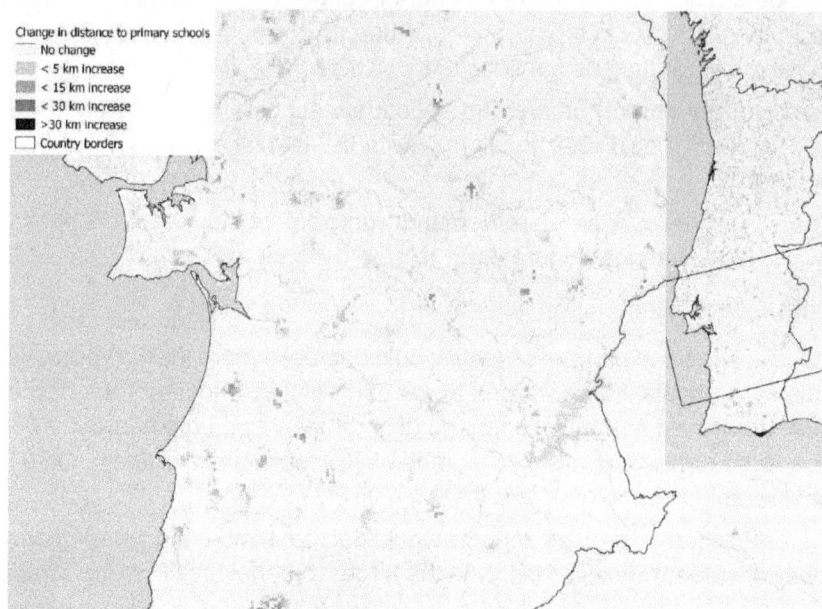

Source: Author's elaboration based on (OECD/EC-JRC, 2021[12])

An alternative policy scenario considers the question: "what if the 2011 school network remains the same in 2035 but student-to-teacher ratios increase everywhere?" The results show that increasing student-to-teacher ratios by 3 more students per teacher reduces annual costs per student by 5%, 12% and 15% in primary schools in sparse rural areas, villages and towns and suburbs, respectively. The impact for secondary schools is uniform across areas, as annual costs per student decrease by 20% in sparse rural areas and by 21% in villages and towns and suburbs.

To further understand the effect of policy choices on future costs and access,

Figure 4.7 displays the comparison between the baseline and the 3 policy scenarios for annual costs per primary (panel a) and secondary (panel b) school students in sparse rural areas.

In primary schools, reorganising the school network to decreased future demand has the effect of preserving similar cost and distance levels to the present scenario, mainly by decreasing the number of high-cost per head small schools that would result from keeping the same network in the future. In contrast, a within-school efficiency policy has the effect of making schools cheaper while preserving the same cost dispersion and distance levels than in 2011.

For secondary schools, the effects of increasing within school efficiency are much more visible, while a policy of school reorganisation maintains annual costs at present levels while slightly increasing travelled distances for the bulk of students (without effect on the general dispersion of travel times).

Figure 4.7. Density of annual cost and distance per primary school student under two different policy scenarios

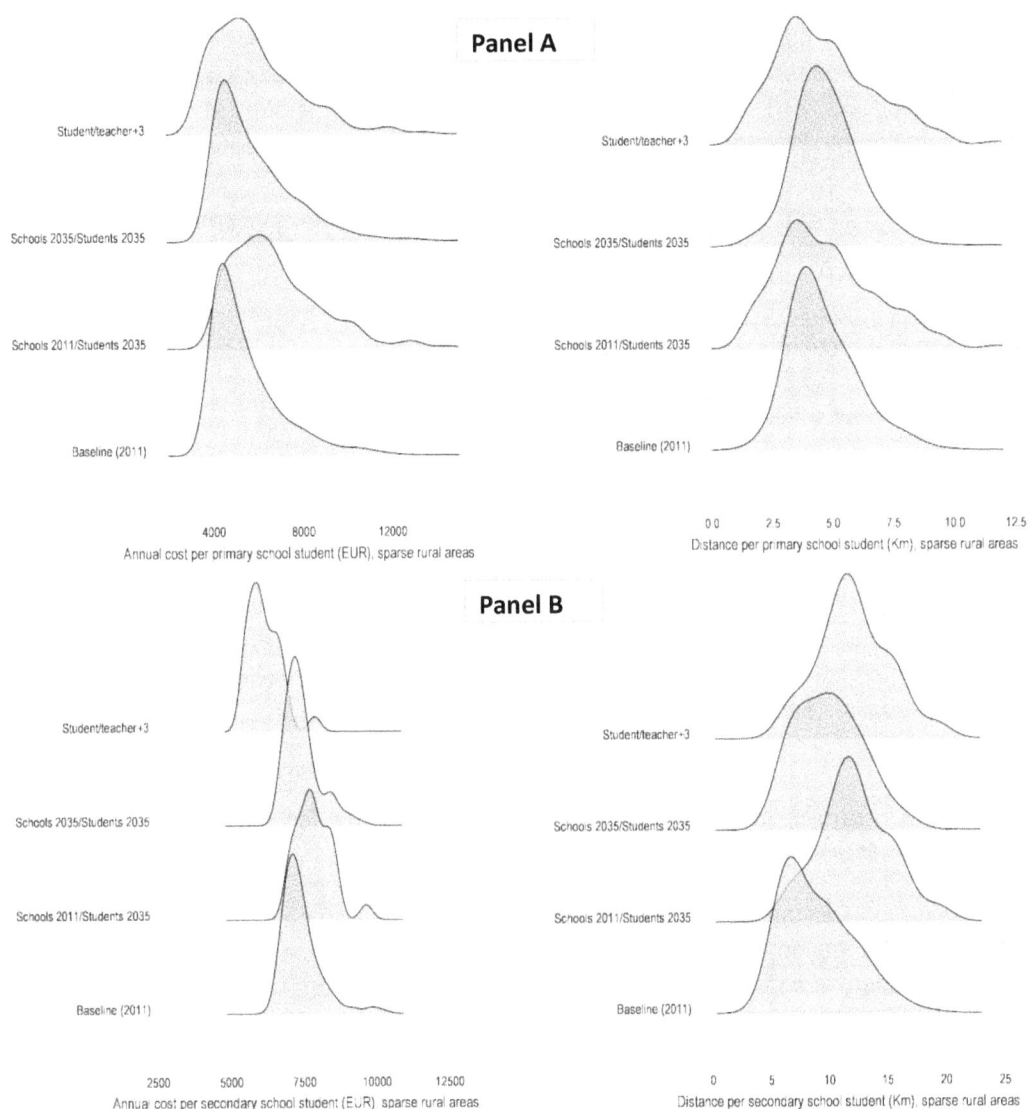

Note: "Schools 2011/Students 2035" corresponds to annual costs and distance per student when the school network of 2011 serves students in 2035; "larger student/teacher ratio" corresponds to the case when student-to-teacher ratios are increased from 13 to 15 students per teacher in primary schools and from 12 to 15 secondary school students per teacher under the "Schools 2011/Students 2035" scenario. Annual costs calculated at schools.
Source: Author's elaboration based on (OECD/EC-JRC, 2021[12])

Recommendations

Demographic changes in Alentejo – with one of the fastest population decline and ageing rates across OECD regions – challenge the provision of education services. These demographic trends imply lower demand for education services and the need to better adapt local public service provision in the region as well as to encourage a better coordination among levels of government. While school consolidation in Portugal has been efficiency-enhancing, school transportation times and costs in remote and sparsely populated areas remain a major challenge in Alentejo. In addition to geographical and demographic factors, inequalities in access to schools across the region are also linked to the local organisation of the transport system. Finally, gaps in digital skills and broadband connectivity present a major challenge that needs to be addressed in order to improve access to education and the organisation of transport.

Further institutional cooperation and involvement of inter-municipal communities (IMCs), a better consideration of local realities to bridge quality and access gaps as well as to improve the geographical mobility of teachers, or policies to reduce digital gaps and potentiate digital services – especially in transport –, could be used to better provide quality educational services throughout the Alentejo region.

Design a specific strategy to bridge quality and access gaps in lagging and remote rural municipalities

Given the fast progression of school consolidation and the already long distances to schools many students face, the national government should pay special attention to designing tailored strategies for small rural municipalities and lagging regions that have failed to improve quality indicators and that have high distances and small schools.

In particular, the national government could undertake cost-benefit analyses that fully take into account the effect of school closures on the accessibility of students living in the most remote areas and associated costs of school transport, even if these do not fall under their responsibility. To this end, the national government or the CCDR Alentejo could commission a dedicated study projecting the financial sustainability of the current model given demographic projections, taking into account structural under-investment in physical infrastructure in these areas. In cases where a new strategy is needed, the government could consider maintaining (or even re-opening) small schools regardless of their size while focusing on quality teaching or piloting alternative transport models with EU or national support as explained below.

Extend municipal strategic planning instruments for school network restructuring to Inter-Municipal Communities

Given the strongly varying local context in Alentejo, municipalities need flexibility to adapt to the effects of demographic change on the school network. Currently, education charters are a municipal strategic planning instrument aimed at reorganising the network of educational and pedagogical facilities. Under the second generation of educational charters, some municipalities have defined and applied their own municipal principles to be followed in the process of reorganising the school network in a way that is more in line with the educational policy defined at local level.

Besides as a way of increasing flexibility, these strategic planning instruments could also be used as vehicle to coordinate actions among neighbouring municipalities. The creation of inter-municipal school network planning instruments, such as inter-municipal education charters, would allow planning beyond municipal administrative boundaries (Santos, Alcoforado and Rochette Cordeiro, 2018[13]). These actions could be undertaken on the framework of increased planning at the level of IMCs.

When planning new school buildings consider co-location and future demand

Many small rural schools struggle with fixed costs including maintenance, repairs and refurbishing of old school buildings. Under-funding for fixed costs since the 2008 financial crisis has resulted in deficient school facilities in some rural municipalities that for instance struggle to offer optimal conditions for students during the summer or winter months (because of lack of heating and/or air conditioning).

Timely decisions on school buildings in rural areas could improve the financial situation of the poorest municipalities while contributing to closing quality gaps. In reconditioning and building new schools, the national government should work closely with municipalities and regions towards innovative models including service co-location (OECD, 2021[9]), and plan strategically the location of new schools based on future demand projections. The cooperation between levels of government on a new model for rural schools is especially relevant in the context of the COVID-19 recovery funds and the digital agenda, as schools can be part of larger digital service hubs in rural communities.

Improve the geographical mobility of teachers while increasing within school efficiency

The ability of Alentejo to design tailored solutions for teacher shortages issues is limited given that teaching responsibilities remain under the full control of the national government. Currently, several teachers are deployed in rural areas by central decision rather than by choice. As a result, many are unfamiliar with the communities where they teach, do not belong to local projects and networks, and ask for a change of location in the following year. The impact of recruitment policies ultimately affects teacher motivation and through this channels feeds into rural-urban gaps in the quality of education.

The government could consider re-evaluating its model of teaching recruitment for rural schools to enhance the participation of municipalities and regions in the process, and ensure a better alignment between needs and motivation. Furthermore, in addition to the opportunities offered by distance learning, the national government should encourage the geographical mobility of teachers – especially young ones – through career incentives (e.g. faster progression of the career system for young teachers), experience-sharing networks by more experienced teachers, and more clear compensation for long travel times. These incentives could be complemented with compensation for long travel times that go beyond financial compensation, including for instance flexible work hours, shorter dedication in classrooms or rotation systems for itinerant teachers, or accommodation support (e.g. teachers' residences).

Further develop transport on demand solutions and increase cooperation between municipalities for the provision of transport

Alentejo local authorities should develop further "*Transporte a pedido*"[6] in the near future, and make the service more dynamic. The provision of Demand-Responsive Transport (DRT) services benefit the entire rural population, from dependent people needing access to basic services, to teachers and upper secondary and vocational students – with more flexible schedules – living in remote areas. DRT initiatives have proven to be effective for school transportation in other countries. In France, "Résa'Tao", the transport on demand service of Orléans metropolis, and "Icilà", the transport on demand service of the urban community of Sophia Antipolis, regularly cover school transport. However, in Alentejo most of the circuits have limited timetables, with one way in the morning and one return in the afternoon or even evening, which does not always accommodate class schedules. The project currently lacks a mobile application and reservations can only be made by phone until 12:30pm on the working day before the day of travel.

The current "*Transporte a pedido*" service could find a way to incorporate existing sophisticated software from the "Résa'Tao" and "Icilà" systems. The software provides users and drivers with reliable and comprehensive real-time information and the possibility to make last-minute bookings from a mobile application or by phone. The routes, the stops and the timing of the service is flexibly adapted based on users demand. The software also has powerful algorithms that take into account itineraries, times and vehicle occupancy rates to optimise every trip, which has led to an increase in the rate of passenger grouping.[7] As the system improves, local authorities should put in place an effective information and marketing strategy to better inform rural inhabitants on these initiatives. The evaluation of the "Grass Routes" service in Wales reported that many local residents were unaware of the service, or thought that the service was not relevant to where they lived, or that it concerned a particular group such as the elderly or disabled (Goodwin-Hawkins, 2020[14]). Transport on demand policies can also be complemented by other measures, such as the provision of an electrically assisted bicycle service, with the deployment of cycle connections, or the full or partial subsidy of driving licences for young people in rural communities.

At the institutional and administrative level, a supra-municipal perspective and greater cooperation between municipalities, inter-municipalities and school clusters could be beneficial for school transport in Alentejo. Such cooperative efforts to improve the transport network already exist in certain sub-regions and should be extended to all the region of Alentejo. This is the case, for example, in Baixo Alentejo and Alto Alentejo, with specific agreements between municipalities and school clusters, or in Montemor-o-Novo in Central Alentejo, where the important role of local parishes in school transport has brought positive results. A better coordination of stakeholders in Alentejo will allow better integration of transport on demand services with regional and national bus networks as well as scaling services from a local to a regional level. CCDR Alentejo should encourage regional transport partnerships across the Alentejo region and provide a space for dialogue between multiple local stakeholders to specifically improve the challenge of school transport, which is key to improving the educational perspectives of Alentejo students, from the youngest to those on vocational training courses.

Develop digital skill plans through cooperation and networks

To support the implementation of the digitalisation of educational services strategy at the national level, the CCDR Alentejo could support the creation of a committee of volunteer teachers to support teachers from rural communities with the most difficulties in their adaptation and training process. Fostering collaboration between teachers has proven to have a positive impact on the use of ICT in classes and on the teaching of digital technologies to students (OECD, 2020[15]). Through a comprehensive and place-based approach, these committees, by following a specific roadmap to 2023, would also ensure that the target of 100% of teachers with digital capabilities by 2023 is achieved specifically in rural areas. These rural committees could also coordinate with the sub-region's Training Centres and their "Digital Ambassadors" in order to assess every six months the difficulties encountered in the field and to ensure targeted follow-up and support for teachers with insufficient levels of digital skills according to the European online self-assessment tool (TET-SAT).

Moreover, in the framework of the national initiative "Portugal INCoDe.2030", networks bringing together employees from digital sectors and teachers could be created in order to review and exchange ideas on the new ICT curriculum guidelines. This interdisciplinary cooperation would better inform students about the broad opportunities offered by digital careers and the digital skills required to access them. This is the case of the Israeli technology incubator MindCET, which promotes collaboration between educational technology developers, schools and teachers to create innovative models for learning with technology. The incubator also offers teachers the opportunity to become edtech entrepreneurs and pilot new innovative pedagogies in their schools. Another example is the Estonian Edulabs programme that enables schools and researchers to develop innovative educational technologies. It also offers an online platform where teachers help each other or consult each other to use technological resources (Burns and Gottschalk, 2020[16]).

Assess and fulfil demand for secondary student accommodation facilities

Establishing a strategy for student accommodation can be an effective alternative to solve the challenges of school transport. A few municipalities in Alentejo have student residences. Some are managed by municipalities and supported by national administration funds (e.g. Serpa, Beja, Almodovar, Portalegre) or will soon be according to the decentralisation programme (Decree-Law no. 21/2019) (e.g. Alcácer do Sal, Odemira).

Accommodating students over 16 years of age during school days would not only avoid daily transport problems, and consequently study performance related issues, but would also allow young people in the region to have a wider educational offer and thus more career opportunities. European Recovery Funds could finance all or part of these residences.

On the other hand, some of the student residences provided by the Ministry of Education throughout the country are not operational due to a lack of demand. The national government could implement a plan to restructure the network of student residences in order to better match supply with demand efficiently and to concentrate student residences where they are most needed.

References

Burns, T. and F. Gottschalk (eds.) (2020), *Education in the Digital Age: Healthy and Happy Children*, Educational Research and Innovation, OECD Publishing, Paris, https://dx.doi.org/10.1787/1209166a-en. [16]

Diário da República (2016), *Resolução do Conselho de Ministros n.º 23/2016*, n.º 70/2016, Série I de 2016-04-11, https://dre.pt/home/-/dre/74094661/details/maximized?p_auth=J4UPdZ4U. [4]

Direção-Geral da Educação (n.d.), *Academia Digital para Pais*, https://www.dge.mec.pt/academia-digital-para-pais. [7]

European Commission/EACEA/Eurydice (2019), *Digital Education at School in Europe*, Eurydice Report, Luxembourg: Publications Office of the European Union, https://eacea.ec.europa.eu/national-policies/eurydice/sites/default/files/en_digital_education_n.pdf. [6]

Goodwin-Hawkins (2020), *Demand Responsive Transport in Rural Areas*, University of Gloucestershire, June 2020, https://doi.org/10.13140/RG.2.2.24576.05124. [14]

Government of Portugal (2020), *Plano de Ação para a Transição Digital de Portugal*, https://www.portugal.gov.pt/gc22/portugal-digital/plano-de-acao-para-a-transicao-digital-pdf.aspx. [5]

Instituto de Avaliação Educativa IP (2019), *Relatorio Nacional PISA Resultados 2018*, https://www.cnedu.pt/content/noticias/internacional/RELATORIO_NACIONAL_PISA2018_IAVE.pdf. [10]

Liebowitz, D. et al. (2018), *OECD Reviews of School Resources: Portugal 2018*, OECD Reviews of School Resources, OECD Publishing, Paris, https://dx.doi.org/10.1787/9789264308411-en. [1]

Liebowitz, D. et al. (2018), *OECD Reviews of School Resources: Portugal 2018*, OECD Reviews of School Resources, OECD Publishing, Paris, https://dx.doi.org/10.1787/9789264308411-en. [2]

OECD (2021), *Delivering Quality Education and Health Care to All: Preparing Regions for Demographic Change*, OECD Rural Studies, OECD Publishing, Paris, https://dx.doi.org/10.1787/83025c02-en. [9]

OECD (2020), *Making the Most of Technology for Learning and Training in Latin America*, OECD Skills Studies, OECD Publishing, Paris, https://dx.doi.org/10.1787/ce2b1a62-en. [15]

OECD (2020), *PISA 2018 Results (Volume V): Effective Policies, Successful Schools*, PISA, OECD Publishing, Paris, https://dx.doi.org/10.1787/ca768d40-en. [11]

OECD/EC-JRC (2021), *Access and Cost of Education and Health Services: Preparing Regions for Demographic Change*, OECD Rural Studies, OECD Publishing, Paris, https://dx.doi.org/10.1787/4ab69cf3-en.   [12]

PNPSE/ DGE (2019), *Relatório PNPSE 2016-2018: Escolas e Comunidades tecendo Políticas Educativas com base em Evidências*, July 2019, https://dspace.uevora.pt/rdpc/bitstream/10174/25940/1/Escolas%20e%20Comunidades%20t ecendo%20Pol%C3%ADticas%20Educativas%20com%20base%20em%20Evid%C3%AAnci as%20%28Relat%C3%B3rio%20PNPSE%202016-2018%29.pdf.   [3]

PORTDATA (2021), *Education data*, https://www.pordata.pt/Tema/Portugal/Educa%c3%a7%c3%a3o-17 (accessed on 1 June 2021).   [8]

Santos, Alcoforado and Rochette Cordeiro (2018), *Os municípios e a educação: os desafios da descentralização para o planeamento da rede escolar*, ResearchGate, January 2018, https://www.researchgate.net/publication/338980757_Os_municipios_e_a_educacao_os_des afios_da_descentralizacao_para_o_planeamento_da_rede_e3A%2F%2Fwww.researchgate. net%2Fpublication%2F338980757_Os_municipios_e_a_educacao_os_desafios_da_descent ralizacao_par.   [13]

Notes

[1] The last two years of secondary education (ages 15-17) include three paths: a) science-humanities courses; b) vocational courses; c) other education and training provision.

[2] Decree-Law no. 55/2018, 6th July and Decree-Law no. 21/2019, 30th January. See https://eacea.ec.europa.eu/national-policies/eurydice/content/portugal_en.

[3] According to the decentralisation law (Decree-Law no. 21/2019), the costs free system is extended from pre-primary to upper secondary education. The funding formula is still under negotiation between central and local authorities.

[4] Portugal was the European country with the highest decrease of the early leave from education and training in Europe, from 2001 to 2020.

[5] Both primary and secondary schools are included although primary schools are more comparable than secondary schools. This case is more comparable than secondary schools. Age ranges in the simulated approach for primary school comprise 6-11 year-olds, so comparatively the actual school data includes an additional year. The split in 3 different paths in secondary schools makes comparisons difficult with simulated secondary schools that consider a single path for students aged 12-18 years-old.

[6] Alentejo launched in 2019 the pilot transport on demand project "*Transporte a pedido*". It has 25 circuits in Baixo Alentejo (Beja, Mértola, Moura), Alentejo Litoral (Odemira) and Alentejo Central (Reguengos de Monsaraz).

[7] Demand-responsive transport services make it easier for people in sparsely populated areas to access health services or their workplaces. This is the case, for example, of Wales, where the "Bwcabus" service has reduced home visits by doctors and average journey times to the nearest employment centre from 52 to 27 minutes (Goodwin-Hawkins, 2020[14]).

Annex A. Degree of urbanisation classification

The Degree of Urbanisation was designed to create a simple and neutral method that could be applied in every country in the world. It relies primarily on population size and density thresholds applied to a population grid with cells of 1 by 1 km. The different types of grid cells are subsequently used to classify small spatial units, such as municipalities or census enumeration areas (see Figure A.1 for an example). The Degree of Urbanisation was endorsed by the UN Statistical Commission in March 2020.[1]

The Degree of Urbanisation classifies the entire territory into:

- Cities, with a population of at least 50 000 in contiguous grid cells with a density of at least 1 500 inhabitants per km^2.
- Dense towns, with a population between 5 000 and 50 000 in contiguous grid cells with a density of at least 1 500 inhabitants per km^2.
- Semi-dense towns, with a population of at least 5 000 in contiguous cells with a density of at least 300 inhabitants per km^2 and are at least 2 km away from the edge of a city or dense town.
- Suburbs, with most of their population in contiguous cells with a density of at least 300 inhabitants per km^2 that are part of a cluster with at least 5 000 inhabitants but are not part of a town.
- Villages, with between 500 and 5 000 inhabitants in contiguous cells with a density of at least 300 inhabitants per km^2.
- Dispersed rural areas, with most of their population in grid cells with a density between 50 and 300 inhabitants per km^2.
- Mostly uninhabited areas, with most of their population in grid cells with a density of less than 50 inhabitants per km^2.

Figure A.1. Degree of urbanisation grid classification around Toulouse, France

Panel A. Grid Panel B. Local units

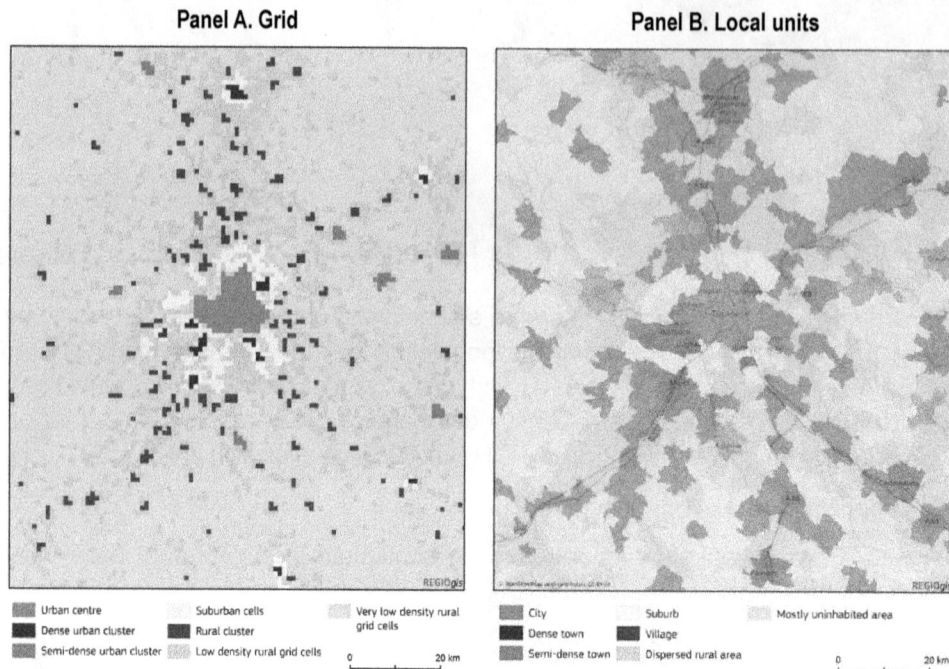

For the analysis in this document, these categories are collapsed into four categories: 1) sparse rural areas (composed of mostly uninhabited areas and dispersed rural areas); 2) villages; 3) towns and suburbs; and 4) cities.

Note

[1] European Commission/ILO/FAO/OECD/UN-Habitat/World Bank (2020), "A recommendation on the method to delineate cities, urban and rural areas for international statistical comparisons", Statistical Commission background document, 51th session, 3-6 March 2020. Items for discussion and decision: demographic statistics. Available at https://unstats.un.org/unsd/statcom/51st-session/documents/BG-Item3j-Recommendation-E.pdf